Transition

Madness 2 Miraculous

NELSON COLÓN

Transition: Madness to the Miraculous

By Nelson Colón / 2nd Edition Revision

U.S. Copyright © 2023 / Library of Congress

Edited and co-written by Nethaniel Nelson Colón

Co-edited by Seth Nelson Colón

New Creation Concepts

ISBN 979-8-218-20636-9

To the **One**
who gave me life, without whom I would have no existence. Who saw
me without form or substance, yet as Psalm 139 speaks of me: "I am
fearfully and wonderfully made."
To the **One** who first saw me, shaped and molded me as He divinely
designed me to be, before I was formed in my mother's womb.
To the **One** who first loved and chose me to be His.
The lover, creator of my soul, breathing life into me.
Without Your love, support and presence in my life, this book would
never have come to be.
You saw me in my formative years, nurturing my dreams and
encouraging my growth. You believed in me before I even believed in
myself, and for that I am forever grateful. Through the ups and downs,
as a faithful Father, You stood by my side, always offering guidance,
love and unwavering faith. You are the pillars of strength in my life.
You are my Life, and I owe all my accomplishments to You!
With every step I took, You were there cheering me on and celebrating
my victories. You have given me the courage to pursue my passions,
and I am eternally indebted to Your belief in me.
Thank you for being a Father to the fatherless.
I sincerely appreciate the privilege of sharing my history, which is
nothing more than Your story about me. You have seen me through
every ordeal in my life and have turned it all around to manifest Your
goodness!
Thank You for being the **Author** of my life's journey,
the **Finisher of my faith**,
and for choosing me before the foundation
of this world.

Foreword

By Nethaniel Nelson Colón

In July 1997, at the age of 13, I deboarded a JetBlue airliner at Orlando International Airport to greet a father I had yet to know. A hug, a handshake, or a smile seemed inappropriate to me, so I greeted him with a wave. It was the first time I would spend time with a father and get to know him truly. I didn't know it then, but it would be the start of a journey, a life-long life-changing relationship. I did not yet know his story, his journey, his peaks, and his valleys. Nor did I understand why he wasn't present during my early childhood, but what I did know is that he loved me and that I could get to know him if I so chose.

The Bible tells the story of Joseph, his trust betrayed by his older brothers. When he had an opportunity to seek vengeance, he instead reassured them that what they did to harm him, "God intended it for good to accomplish what is now being done." {Genesis 50: 20}

This book is what is now being done.

It is the product of decades of tears, smiles, joys, hopes, hurts, and healing. I hope it finds you at a point in your life where life weighs heavily when it's hard to see the purpose in pain. What many people think is intended to kill them is the very thing that God will use to save them. I pray this book would be a conduit for hope and change in your own life as it chronicles the hope and change that is pervasive in my father's life.

Accolades to my firstborn *Nethaniel Nelson*, who teaches English and Humanities at Cambria Heights Academy High School in Hollis Queens, NY.

Thank you, son, for assisting me in this labor of love,
and helping to mold my story for God's glory.

We've laughed, cried, and bonded more closely together in the undertaking of this endeavor. Appreciate you "Showing" my story and helping my narrative come to life.

I am genuinely thankful and incredibly proud of you. You've grown into the man of valor, loving husband, and faithful father that I have always aspired to be. You are the first arrow in my quiver, and you have already exceeded my expectations in hitting the mark. I love you son; May our Heavenly Father continue to bless you and use you mightily for His glory.

Nelson Colón

KUDOS!

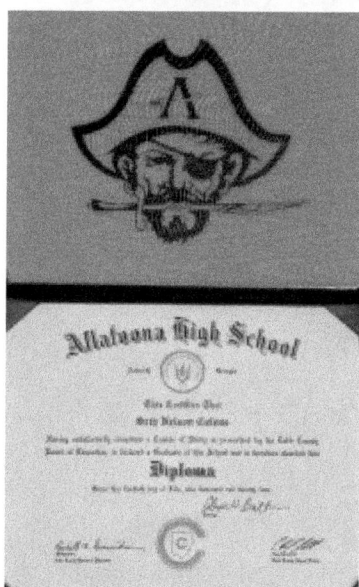

Introduction

Birth & Rebirth

The last phase of the first stage of labor is imminent with cervical dilation of 8 to 10 CM. Medical experts claim that this is the most painful process as the baby has positioned itself in the birth canal of the mother and is beginning to crown and push itself through to be birthed.

In comparison, our lives are inundated with traumatic events; pain can be the one constant in our lives that we come to expect and even count on. I share my story asking that you take heart in knowing that as we are being prepared and positioned for that last **transitioning phase**, as we near the end of the labor process, at the end of that dark tunnel, is a magnificent blinding light, and a great release when you are born and reborn.

Transition must strive ever higher, aspiring toward transcension.

Transcendence through the Spirit naturally leads to transformation.

Transformation through Christ, inevitably, brings forth

Transfiguration.

In this spiritual journey from transition to transcension, we are invited to embrace the transformative power of prayer, allowing it to lead us toward a profound and lasting change in our lives. **Through our union with Christ**, we can eventually experience the epitome and embodiment of transfiguration. Which brings us closer to our true nature and purpose, reflecting the divine image in which we were initially created for. It is my prayer that the vivid images of my story will stay with you and that my testimony will assist you on the personal road that you too must travel to reach your own ultimate spiritual destination.

Chapter One

"Rosebud"

The name that tumbled from the lips of a dying Orson Welles in *Citizen Kane,* * to this day holds an especially poignant meaning for me. For Welles, that one word illustrated how all the riches that he had amassed as a wealthy newspaper publisher had never brought him happiness. No, his inner hopes and dreams resided in the childhood sled that was carelessly tossed into a fire. For him, this was the death of innocence and the carefree childhood that brought him a joy he could never quite recapture. Although a sled was at the heart of that 1941 Academy Award-winning movie, my Rosebud was a tricycle. Many people find it hard to recall much before the age of four or five, but I remember it as if a recent dream, as a three-year-old, — anxiously awaiting sunrise.

** Credit to **Ken Walker** (Freelance Writer / Charisma Magazine) for editing this initial intro. "Thanks Ken!"*

I would wake before the sun and await the cock's crow. By 5 am, streaks of light would break the night sky. That was my signal, I would soon be free to ride. My two tricycles weren't kept in the house. I tried that once and received a swift slap from my mother's chancleta. [1] I kept them by the marquesina [2] at the top of our driveway. Marquesinas were usually used to store a car or hang a hammock and host visitors; I remember the neighbors using them for such. For us, it had long lost its original purpose. It had become somewhat crowded; its contents were rust-worn blue coal grill with one leg missing, a spotted mattress laid against its back post, several dented toolboxes spilling over with wrenches, nuts, and bolts strewn upon the concrete floor, painted over gray so many times I'm sure my father lost count. With the sky still purple black, I would stand there staring at my trikes. One was red with a cold metallic seat and the other a black rusted color with a vinyl seat. I found the black one appealing because it was a "big boys" trike. It was taller with longer, higher handlebars. It was a smoother ride because my dad had oiled the wheels recently, but the thought of my arms aching from reaching up to grasp the bars all day made me default to my red trike. I used to tell my mom that I wasn't too big for it, but the truth was I didn't want to be rid of it because the color made me go faster.

TRANSITION

A rooster has a way of instinctively knowing when the first bit of red and orange is going to appear amidst the horizon. As soon as he commenced crowing his "Wake-Up" call, I was off to the races. I threw my leg over the trike, checked the front wheel spokes for my Topps Mickey Mantle, and rolled down the driveway. I couldn't peddle just yet; the sound of the rusty petals might alert my parents, but once I was on the street, I was free to pick up speed and pedal hard. I would push as hard as I could and try not to fidget out of fear the seat might squeak. My mother later told me that I was the talk of the town, "There's that Cotto kid on his rusty bike again" they'd say, "Coño, his father can't oil that damn seat?" They didn't have disposable pampers then; they were cloth diapers that my mother would have to wash by hand. I don't think there was any Downy then, so maybe the diapers felt rough and uncomfortable, or maybe I just didn't like feeling constricted. Whatever the reason, I couldn't leave my diapers on for too long. I would ride butt-naked, donning only my dingy white toddler t-shirt. The metal seat would eventually cook under the tropical sun, burning my bare behind. The downhill breeze was soothing; it caressed my naked body with friendly warmth. Coasting down each hill was glorious; a more than adequate reward for the effort it took to climb one. A warm wind was blowing my hair back.

The only thing I had to remember was to keep my mouth closed while speeding downward. It was nasty when you got a mouth full of gnats. My calves would cramp as I pedaled my way uphill. Sweat built across my forehead and would soak my eyebrows. It was only a matter of time until it would drip into my eye. This was my motivation. I would push hard to the top of each hill before a bead of sweat would sting my eye. Sometimes I would beat it, other times I wasn't so fortunate and had to ride with one eye closed for a while, cringing as I passed by the early risers.

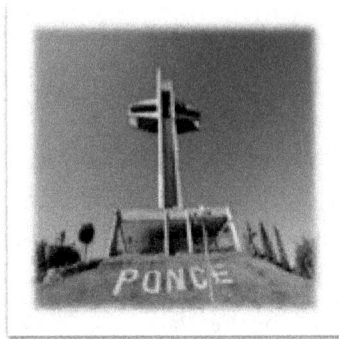

I could see some people in their windows turning on their lights and putting their dented metal coffee pots on their grease-stained stoves. The air smelled of fresh coffee and boiled milk. Round and round I'd go. There were only about ten houses on my street. I would ride to the end of the street and turn back, passing my house as fast as possible, hoping to impress Mami. At times, I remember stopping at the end of the street and pulling my trike into the grass to get a view of the valley, and the town of Machuelo in the distance. My home was at the top of a mountain, or maybe it was just a big hill, but to me, it was like looking down from Machu Picchu. I would realize how minuscule the town beneath me was. I claimed ownership; Ponce and Machuelito were mine.

My trikes would occupy my entire day, but I would make sure to stop by the house to watch for "Papi" to leave in the late morning. I was afraid he would make me come back in, so I would park across the street. Usually, my older brother, Cano, at eight years of age, would sit idly in the marquesina as if he didn't have to get ready for school, watching the streets for his friends. Lillian was the oldest, an official teenager at thirteen, and operated more like a mother than an older sister, scrambling to prepare lunch for everyone. Even my father looked and yelled at her in a similar fashion to our mom. At nine years old, Veronica never seemed to wake early enough to see him leave, closed in her room. But not me, I liked watching as he drove off in his black '55 Chevy. The red interior was so torn you could see patches of yellow

6

scattered throughout. If he saw me, I was sure to wave. Sometimes I was acknowledged when he motioned his cigarette at me. Once he left, there wasn't much that helped me distinguish how much time went by. I stayed out all day. My mother would call me to give me some water and bread. She would put my diaper back on, but that only lasted one trip down the street. The sun would start to set, and a cool breeze would start to speak through the trees.

That is when I started recognizing Papi' s distinct style of yelling, "Mira, este muchacho está afuera enud, Carajo!" [3] When I heard those words I would pull into the driveway, dump my trike amongst the tools, and go back into the house. Mami would find me and address my nakedness, but my relentless yearning to feel free and unconstricted would eventually outwit Mami's distinctiveness for overprotection.

One incident that took place during this same period of my life that further added to my emotional instability was when I almost had myself castrated. * In the re-enactment of Mister Magoo, opening my mother's umbrella, and attempting to use it as a parachute, I jumped off the bed and yelled out, "Mister Magoo!" When my genitalia got caught and slashed by a sharp hardened piece of torn vinyl jetting out of the upholstery of an old chair right by my mother's bed. Lillian was cleaning the metal window blinds in my mother's bedroom and was utilizing the kitchen chair to stand on. It happened so quickly I didn't even feel the pain until I looked down and saw my young manhood hanging from a thread of vein and flesh. For the fear of getting a spanking, I didn't even yell. I just gently cupped it with my hands. I walked about the house that way, for a while, without anyone noticing what had happened to me. I must have been in some sort of shock. Incredibly, I faintly recall contemplating whether I should finish ripping off the remaining piece, put on a band-aid, and just hope that my mother wouldn't notice. At that instant, my brother Cano saw me, and let out a yell, "MAMI!" My mother came running, and when she saw blood oozing out through my little fingers, holding on to my private parts, she topped my brother's yell with a shrill scream straight out of a horror movie. Wrapping me up in a towel and an old quilt, she picked me up and ran hysterically out of the house. Desperately looking for someone to help get me to the hospital, she finally convinced a neighbor of the urgency, who then took us in his car.

Thank GOD, they got me to the hospital in time to save my jewels as well as the future Colón family. Blessed with two normal healthy sons. Well, three. *Nehemiah Nelson* who was stillborn, graduated heaven-bound, getting his wings prematurely, being spared the traumas and testings of this life.

TRANSITION

* In Hindsight, the devil tried to rob me of my bloodline, but God began training me even then, when I was totally oblivious to Him, that **"No Weapon formed against me would prosper."** *Even during my birth, the devil, who comes only to rob, kill, and destroy, tried to end my life. My mother who experienced many difficulties during labor almost lost me, not to mention almost lost her life, ushering me into this* **purgatory.**

Looking back, my three-wheelers represented much more than fun and recreation. Three years later I missed those days in Puerto Rico. I was six years old and found myself in Brooklyn. The house we came to live in belonged to my Titi[4] Gladys, my mother's sole younger sister. She was beautiful; fair with the striking contrast of black curly hair and crimson heart-shaped lips. She married Uncle Pete, a former Marine combat veteran from the Korean War who always reeked of cigars. I could hear the "QJ" train from my bedroom window as its wheels screeched on the tracks just a block away on Broadway. I often sat on the front porch of the house, looking up Himrod Street, like my brother once did in Ponce.

I would wait for my best friend Victor and his sister Sonia to come down from their adjoining house on 25 Himrod to play tag with them. Or better yet, I would watch for the ten-year-old girls who went to P.S. 274. They would walk by in groups or with their parents at around 8 o'clock in the morning and again when school let out at three. I couldn't wait to start attending. I had just celebrated my 6th birthday, skipped over kindergarten, and began First Grade the following semester. My most vivid memory came on a day when I found myself grieving for my trikes again. I was sitting on the porch waiting for Grandma to call me in for dinner, watching kids playing Chinese handball off the wall of Menorah's Nursing Home across the street.

A young teenage boy passed by on his Schwinn bicycle. I found myself admiring the bright red metallic color and how the sun gleamed off it, mesmerizing me with memories of my small red trike. On previous occasions, I had commented on it as he rode by. On this day, he stopped outside the front gate. I had never talked to him before. I wanted to know "Where did he get it, and how did it feel to ride it?" Was he friendly enough to let me try it? I thought. He must have read my mind, "Want a ride?" he asked.

9

I remembered my mother had been warning me never to leave the front porch, but I couldn't resist the offer. Since I was too small to ride a two-wheeler by myself, he offered to put me on the frame right before him. "What the heck, I thought mustering up some courage, "Okay!" I responded, not giving it, another thought as I hopped up onto the front handlebar. I thought to myself, he'll ride me around the block and have me back in no time; No one will even miss me. Halfway around the block, however, he stopped. "Hey, I've got to get something for my bike," he said. "What?" I inquired. "A pump, you're too heavy. I won't be able to take you back without it." he retaliated. Immediately feeling anxious, I protested, "I've got to get back before my grandma misses me." "Hey, it won't take long. C'mon, this is where I live." We entered a dirty, broken-down building with graffiti scribbled around the front door. I reluctantly followed the boy down the hallway, which stunk of urine. At the end of the hall was a door leading to the basement and I hesitated at the top of the stairs as he fumbled around for the light. Finally finding the switch he turned it on and said, "C'mon down, there's nothing to be afraid of!"

I followed him down the stairs. He started looking around like he was searching for something and urged me to come to help him. As he looked around, he stopped at an old washing machine in the corner of the dusty basement. His next words sounded rehearsed and inextricably incited a sense of apprehension as he said, "I think I found the pump for my bike, but it's pinned behind this washing machine, can you help me get it out?" I didn't know what else to do except see where he was pointing. He was motioning his hand at a spot behind the washer. As I approached the washer, he stopped me right in front of it and told me to bend down and reach through the other side of the washer, since I was smaller. As I bent down to try to see the pump, which I hadn't fully realized was imaginary, he grabbed ahold of me. Brought my pants and briefs down to my ankles and pinned me against the machine.

TRANSITION

My eyes fixed on a rusty groove the movement of the washer had dug into the cement floor. I thought about my rosebud-the red trike and its shorter handlebars that didn't hurt to reach-as he assured me, he wouldn't hurt me. I remembered how I needed to be careful not to fidget or the seat of the trike would squeak, as he held my head down and violently shook behind me. As he groaned, and eventually let out a strong sigh of what seemed relief, I remembered waving to my father as he pulled away in his black Chevy, wondering if he would approve of what was happening. He released me and told me to pull up my pants. I slowly began to do so but couldn't bring myself to turn around or look at the boy. The memory of my trikes seemed more distant as I heard him begin to ascend the basement steps. Finally able to unfreeze from the spot he had left me in, I commenced following him up the stairs.

I didn't quite understand what had happened, as I was too young to fully comprehend it. Somehow, instinctively, I felt dirty. The boy quickly dropped me off at the corner and made me walk the rest of the way home. As I came through the gate my sister Vero opened the front door asking me where I had been, "You know you're not supposed to leave the stoop." I didn't answer and just went straight to the bathroom to wash up. As I sat down my grandma served me a plate of piping hot rice and beans. My mom had just got home. She kissed me on my head and asked me why I wasn't eating, "Come muchacho, se te enfria la Comida!" [5] I began eating my food quietly. I believed that I reaped the consequence of my disobedience. My mother had told me not to stray away from the front porch. It was my fault, or so I thought at the time. For more than thirty years I locked away that awful truth somewhere deep and hidden; treating it like some bad dream that I would hopefully soon forget.

It has since been a closely guarded secret until now.

Chapter Two

Belittled Beginnings

My mother conceived me toward the end of the blistering heat wave of '57 and was put on bed rest for the first four months of her pregnancy. A sentence she did not take well, despite the pain and discomfort. She would much rather wade throughout the house, performing her usual daily tasks at quarter speed, than be left alone with her thoughts, staring at the cracks in the ceiling of her bedroom my father would never spackle. I think it was hardest for her to "temporarily" leave work, knowing her job was not guaranteed when she would return. She also knew the stress and pace of the factory sweatshop in the Bowery would not end well for me, so inevitably she had to quit while she carried me. During this time, the only thing my mother could manage to do was cook while my oldest sister Lilly, just 10, handled the cleaning and laundry. Almost every day she would make her usual but delicious yucca and bacalao.[6] Her diet almost always consisted of Vianda:[7] yucca, sauteed fried onions, and mojo[8], mixed with olive oil and bacalao. She loved dipping tostones[9] into a mojito sauce.[10]

That guilty pleasure was transferred intravenously to me. She would hardly leave the house until the day my soon-to-be-father saw fit to throw my pregnant mother down a flight of stairs. I can't help but suspect it was an attempt on our lives. She had been carrying me for six months. When Lilly recalls the incident, still traumatized to this present day, can just vaguely depict the graphic details. My mother's desperate attempt to flee from my father's explosive violent outburst must have sent her body reeling down the stairs from our fourth-floor apartment. As she flailed her arms with futility grasping for the wooden railing endeavoring to cease her descent, only to succeed in skipping a few steps before the left side of her face and shoulder took the full brunt of the final four steps.

Instead, when Veronica and Cano recall the story, they remember looking out to see if our mother had safely escaped the building. As their limited attention span was quickly diverted by the thick frost that layered our only window. They watched a single snowflake descend, melting into the glimmering white virgin snow below, blanketing vehicles along Broome Street.

Late that afternoon he had come home after he had been missing for two days. He reeked of sex and rum. My mother's inquiry into his whereabouts infuriated him so much that he decided to make it clear that he didn't want to talk about it. My mother awoke minutes later at the bottom of the steps to our floor, of the 4-story tenement building at 171 Broome. No medical professional could say with any certainty what effect such an incident might have had on an unborn child other than death. However, recent medical studies do claim that singing and caressing the belly while a child is still in the womb strengthens the eventual emotional bond between caregiver and infant. For that reason, I believe the sound of my mother's voice kept me alive as she held her belly with quivering hands and sang to me while being transported by a mini ambulance to Gouverneur Hospital.

"Los pollitos dicen pío, pío, pío cuando tienen hambre, cuando tienen frío. La gallina busca el maíz y el trigo les da la comida y les presta abrigo. Bajos sus alas acurrucaditas hasta el otro día duermen los pollitos." [11]

(The chicks say, "Peep, Peep, Peep", when they are hungry and when they are cold. The mother hen looks for corn and wheat, provides them with food, and shelters them. Under her wings, the little chicks huddle up and sleep until the next day.)

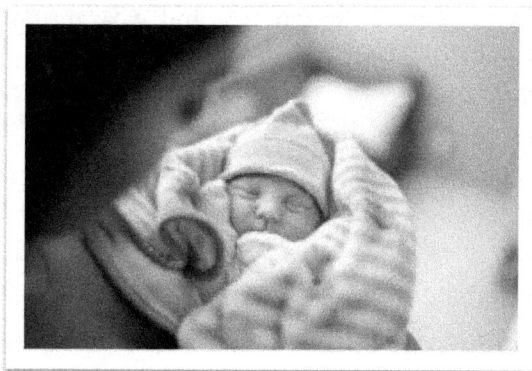

We both survived. Three months after her "accident," my mother found herself back in the same hospital she had shambled up to half-a-dozen times for similar "accidents." My father's actions must have had a cumulative effect because my mother experienced considerable difficulty during labor. I pictured myself, comically, as an unborn child holding onto her placenta for dear life, not wanting to leave the warm safe confines of her womb.

The ten-hour process nearly killed her. Two hours shy of midnight, the maternity wing was finally filled with our tangled cries in room 305. Two doors down from where the same doctor examined my mother's injuries during her last visit. I was **clothed in blood**, so much so that the nurse and doctor had to seek each other's gaze to affirm that it was cause for panic. After I was cleaned, my mother was stable enough to see me but not hold me. Dr. Rabinowitz tentatively handed me over to my Uncle Pete a.k.a. "Pelly" who recalled; as he would remind me time and time again, of the story of him being there, in my father's absence. Dropping the dime on my dear old Dad, "Tité", as they referred to him, saying he was too busy dancing and galavanting that night to welcome me into the world. Thus, my Uncle Pete became my unofficial God-father figure.

My mother went home the next day, to a tenement adjacent to the local grocer's warehouse. Living in the Lower East Side of Manhattan allotted my father plenty of unstable temp labor, but none paid well. Inevitably my mother became the main breadwinner having experience in the industrial Singer sewing machines. Still, due to the severity of my mother's traumatic labor pushing me into this world, she could not immediately return to work. She would walk all the way to the factory from Broome Street, via Delancey Street, and onto the Bowery just to save her bus fare. At the Textile Mill, my mother did piecework as a seamstress but was not allowed the title. Not her. An immigrant? A woman? A Spanish speaker? If she asked, they would never answer with anything but a question.

"A promotion?" You might as well say we could place a man on the moon. Most women received $50 a week but my mother made closer to $75 doing "piece work", working in a sewing room on the fifth floor for ten hours a day. She was docked pay when she had to use the restroom so her first stop when she got home was always the toilet. Windows littered most of the walls, but most were too warped by heat and time to allow a view of the outside; even if they did all you would see were the brick walls of another building. She often complained about the army of fans failing to provide any relief from the summer heat; "merely stirring the cauldron," as she would put it. She didn't talk much about work, but I noticed her calloused and cracked fingertips; fingernails black and green from blood clots caused by deep needle pricks. I liked it when her hands were especially purple, usually because a needle broke off in her finger or palm. This meant she couldn't hit me and my brother for a while.

My mother was a regular Norma Ray; a "Guerrera" warrior queen. The local newspaper did a piece on her efforts to organize a union at her job. She even refused to take welfare, claiming it only made the poor lazy and weak. With four kids, she could have easily joined the lines by the local office and got her government portion; bricks of cheese, butter, canned meat, and milk, but she would rather work for her money. Despite her fighting spirit, she grew tired of both my father and life on the Lower East Side. For my father, the living and working conditions in New York were the perfect justification for his increased agitation and abuse. For this reason, my mom eventually asked to move back to her "Isla de mi infancia."[12] Surprisingly, my father embraced the idea. He and my mother always dreamed of opening a little coffee shop or "Cafetin" in their old neighborhood of Ponce. My mother hoped it would be a reset and a new start, but my father would ensure it was more of the same. A lime green house awaited us in Ponce; primed to be filled with new and hopefully finer memories.

I liked licking the walls because I convinced myself they tasted like lollipops. Once I nearly received a swift slap across the back of my neck, but my father was too drunk to swat with any accuracy. He claimed the tropical air exacerbated his alcoholism, drinking most of his income. We lived small in the Big Apple and hoped to live bigger in Puerto Rico. But as we all soon realized, *the road to hell is indeed paved with good intentions.*[13]

While I explored the island naked on my trikes my family tried as best they could to enjoy the time when my father wasn't home. My mother would spend hours sewing, keeping her skills up. She created most of the clothes we wore dresses, overalls, jumpers, and my favorite, guayaberas[14]. I saw her smile most when she was creating something new. I remember when she made me my favorite blanket; she used scraps from all her projects to piece together a patchwork sheet for me. I would lay it out in the front yard for picnics to imagine I sailed a vexed sea or traveled the globe aboard a rainbow. I would imagine I was Aladdin on my magic carpet ride. In the evening, on my father's drive home from the Cafetin, we would await the sound of his old Chevy muffler. It was rusted clean through, a hole the size of my father's fist had aged through it. His approach could be heard from a distance. The sound of him pulling into the driveway stripped smiles from everyone's faces including mine.

When he would enter the house, everyone was slapped with a deafening silence. My brother and sisters' fearful stares would shift from him to me and then back to him again until he usually broke the silence with a complaint. He never liked what my mother prepared for dinner. On this day, my mother prepared a fresh pot of pollo guisado[15] which he seemed to take pleasure in calling "hog food." On occasion, he would even heave it onto our front porch. She would fetch the top portion that didn't touch the ground and still serve him the best pieces. When we did eat together at the table, resembling a modern family, he would ramble on and on, slurring half his words as he ate. Most of the words he spoke were indecipherable or expletives which I was supposed to try to ignore. The one word he would repeat clearly was "la Maquina!" It was like clockwork, as soon as he finished eating, he would start his search for the sewing machine. My mother would move it almost every day. But she was sure not to hide it; that would only upset him further.

TRANSITION

When he found it he would pace around the house with it in hand; mother pleadingly, following him. There was one episode when my mother had screwed it onto the table on the back porch. He pulled on it for so long that we started to think mom finally beat him, but the plastic table eventually snapped in two. Off it went and strewn across the backyard. It would lay there till he fell asleep. She couldn't wait till the morning, for the dew would rust it and make its repair even more impossible. If it wasn't too late and we were still up, we would have helped her pick up the pieces. Lillian, Veronica, and my brother Jose (nicknamed "Cano" because of his dirty-blonde hair) would work on it, like a jigsaw puzzle, with our mom for hours, days, and weeks, trying to put it back together again. As my brother and sisters gave up on the project, Mami would keep tinkering. I would watch her as her eye's shone glossy, water flooding her lower eyelids. When she thought I wasn't looking she would let them overflow and roll down her cheeks. I didn't understand until much later what the machine meant to her; it was her last inch of pride, the only means to provide any kind of life for us. At times I would stand by the doorway of her room and study her efforts to repair her dignity. When she noticed I was watching her she would call me over, sit me on her lap and say, "it's nothing, don't worry papito."

She should've been a mechanic; her magical use of scotch and duct tape, screws, and needles eventually proved successful. Unfortunately, it seemed like as soon as it was fixed it would just take another trip outside. When my father was home, their loud voices easily penetrated the thin walls. At times, when it escalated to objects crashing, I would purposefully walk in on them, hoping to give her some rest. Usually, I would remain unseen, but I remember a time when their eyes locked on me for a second. I stared back at them, frozen in my shoes, wishing it would end, but anxious to see what would come next. I had the bright idea to qualify my presence and so I asked for juice. My father's soot-covered hand met my face and before I knew what had happened my mother was taking me up from the floor. I remember thinking, 'all I asked for was juice' as my mother took me out of the room and my father's yells followed us, "There's no damn juice!"

21

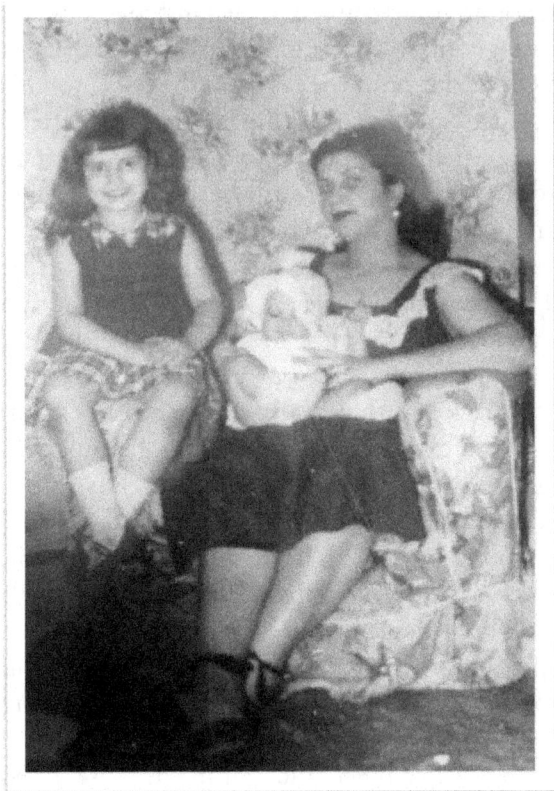

When night fell, my mother would tell us to go to bed as she cleaned and recleaned the house. I would drift to sleep to the sound of my mother wiping the dining room table. There were splotches of rust that could never be removed without throwing out the entire table, but that didn't stop her from trying to wipe them clean. Later, as she got older, they called it O.C.D., but I knew better, as it was the way she coped with life. It was later that I realized she didn't want to go to bed. She couldn't, before she was able to shut the door, I could hear him start in on her, asking where she was and not caring to even let her answer before he cursed her further. P.R. only lasted two years, as in the mid-Summer of 1963, we moved back to New York.

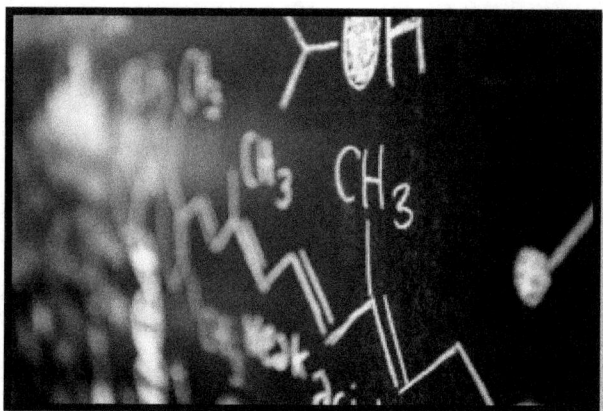

Einstein is said to have claimed that the very *"definition of insanity is doing the same thing over and over and expecting different results."*

Hence, my mother left 'La Isla del Encanto'[16] without my father this time for yet another restart, this time in Bushwick. Nothing could be worse than the Lower East Side.
Or could it?

Chapter Three

The Golden Rules

Rule 1: Stay Clean

We lived at Titi [17] Gladys and Uncle Pete's house, 23 Himrod Street, for nearly three years, before I was old enough to commence grade school. For the first year, my days mostly consisted of waiting anxiously for my oldest sister Lilly to get home from the Five & Ten she worked part-time on Broadway in Brooklyn. She knew I would be waiting so she'd always made sure to have a nickel mini-toy or some Bazooka Bubble Gum in her purse.

I faintly recall seeing her crying one day as she arrived home from work, having forgotten to bring me a treat. As a matter of fact, everyone was crying in the house, as the family were all gathered around the television set watching the news. So, there I was, a five-year-old kid, trying to make sense of the chaos. It turned out the President got shot during some parade. I couldn't wrap my head around why everyone, not just my family but also folks on the news, was shedding tears for a man I didn't even know. They kept talking about him being a good man and a great President, referring to him as JFK. A few years later, another tragedy struck the Kennedy family when I heard about his younger brother, Robert, who had also been shot and killed. *

*Both Kennedy assassinations had a profound impact on the United States. President John F. Kennedy's death on November 22, 1963, marked the end of an era referred to as "Camelot" and had implications for civil rights, the Cold War, and American foreign policy. Robert F. Kennedy's assassination on June 5, 1968, in the midst of his presidential campaign, was a tragedy that many believed could have altered the course of American politics. These assassinations occurred during a tumultuous time in American history, marked by the civil rights movement, anti-war protests, and much social upheaval.

Eventually, I turned my attention to watching children my age and older pass the house on their way to and from Public School 274. It wasn't until September of 1965 that I was old enough to join the ranks. The day before my first day of school, I went to bed but couldn't sleep. I left the window open and pulled my quilt to my chin, hoping the cool air would help, but the persistent pounding in my chest proved too loud. The screech of train tracks called out to me from less than a mile away. When I finally did drift into unconsciousness, I woke up in what seemed to be only minutes but was, in fact, hours; my mother pacing in and out of my room repeating "¡Hoy es el día, Levántate! No quieres llegar tarde a tu primer día de escuela."[18] Dragging myself out of bed, I felt nervous anxiety mingled with a gaseous stomach on the brink of nausea. Before I could even wash up or brush my teeth, my mother was fitting me with the new clothes she had purchased for my first day of school. As she did, she gently enforced rule number 1: "Be careful not to get your new clothes dirty." I complied by avoiding the puddles crossing the street and trying not to plant my new PF Flyers on any dog poop that seemed strategically placed along the sidewalk. It was like the game I played when mom took me to the supermarket, "don't step on the cracks you'll break your mama's back." I lagged my mother. From afar, I'm sure it looked like I didn't know how to walk; jumping from left to right, onto the grass, then onto the street. She was patient. She knew I was only trying to follow rule number 1. She even pulled me away, saving me from a mound of excrement left by someone carelessly not curbing their dogs, "Cuidado!" [19]

When we arrived at the front of P.S. 274, we saw the masses working their way to the "playground." It was more of a parking lot, concrete from end to end. Grass in general seemed like a luxury not worth the expense. Past the rusty gates and painted floor squares, we went, as we found ourselves navigating the crowd via non-verbal cues and arrows tapped to the side of the school building.

Eventually, we arrived at a fancy man. At this point, there was no more hiding the fact that my mother knew only a handful of words in English. I could've helped, but I was afraid to talk to him for fear I might say something wrong. So instead, we nodded yes to everything he said. This got us to a white woman who knew

enough Spanish to take us to a line of first graders inside the building.

As I made it through the crowds, I was sure to watch my feet so no one would unintentionally step on my new PF Flyers. This was before I learned about STOMPSIES from my peers. That would be the end of my white flyers. My mom appeared as nervous as I felt inside, her eyes darting around the cafeteria. She turned to me and said in Spanish, "Remember, today is going to be very special for you. This is a day you will never forget. So, make sure you get everything right." "Everything right?" I thought. The distraught look on her face made my stomach contort in my ribcage. She must have realized she only had a few more minutes with me, so she quickly spewed out seven very important rules that I had no more than a second to memorize:

"Stay Clean", she said.

I knew that one already.

"Obey the Teacher"

Who's the teacher, the fancy man, or that white woman over there?

"Don't Talk"

Why would I?

"Be Kind"

Aren't I always?

"Pay Attention"

Doesn't everybody?

"Don't Run"

Why? Will someone be chasing me?

"Do your Best"

But what if my best wasn't good enough?

"You be a good boy now," she said as if I needed more reminders. The idea of being left at the mercy of a total stranger scared me out of my wits so I held tighter when she tried to pull away. She reinforced "Make Mama proud!" as she kissed me one more time and broke free of my death grip. I fought my tears as she walked away and blew a few final kisses at me. I couldn't believe she was gone. How could she leave me? Next, a strange old woman with gray hair and thick-rimmed glasses led me away. I carried the same blank, rather helpless stare to the crowds of new, freshly scrubbed faces. I didn't know any of these kids, though they seemed to know each other. It was probably the consequence of not attending kindergarten. I wondered why I was so much bigger than most-I didn't know then, but I was already seven when most of them were still only six. A white woman introduced herself as Mrs. Hoffman. She had us line up in two lines, one for girls and the other one for boys. I wondered if it was normal to have only 10 boys to a whopping 23 girls. What did they do with the rest of the boys? Was I next? Our classroom didn't fit us; three of us didn't have desks or chairs but it didn't seem to bother anyone else. Mrs. Hoffman spoke softly so I just followed along and mimicked what everyone else was doing so as not to seem stupid: "Place your jacket and book bag beneath the coat hooks. Snack bags go by the back window." But I didn't have one. "And you don't go anywhere near the teacher's desk."

Rule 2: Obey The Teacher

After being systematically situated in what was to be our permanent seating arrangement for the year, my teacher began her opening speech; "Good morning, Class. Welcome to P.S. 274. My name is Mrs. Hoffman, and I'm going to be your first-grade teacher."

She had each one of us stand and quickly say our names, and then began lecturing us on the dos and don'ts; "Please feel free to ask any questions, but first wait until I'm finished, then raise your hand." She seemed nice enough. Smiled a lot, with excited eyes that seemed to smile. I felt like raising my hand immediately to tell her that my mother had already told me all I needed to know, but I restrained myself. I wanted to see if my mother had left anything out. By this time, the pains in my intestines had changed. I was still nervous, but they were accompanied by cramps. I tried to ignore it. I kept telling myself, "She said to wait till she was finished talking," whispering it as I started to grip my stomach. "Obey your teacher," I thought.

I couldn't ask to go. As minutes went by and her mouth continued to move, I cared less about what she had to say. I wanted to ask to go, but as soon as I got the nerve to raise my hand she immediately interjected, "Oh yes, and it's very important that you make sure to 'Go' and use the bathroom at home before coming to school, to prevent anyone from disrupting our morning schedule." She sternly warned that everyone would have to wait until eleven o'clock, just before lunch, before being allowed to go to the bathroom.

"Obey your teacher!" I cringed. "I don't want to ruin the morning schedule." I was doomed; it was only 9:00 a.m. I desperately hoped that some other kid would have the nerve to break the ice and ask to go, but no one did. So, I just waited and hoped that eleven o'clock would hurry up and roll around. I waited and waited and waited... but the more I stared at the clock the less it seemed to move, "Obey your teacher."

It felt like an eternity. myself up as best I could, although the smell had already permeated my pants. At one point the pain became so unbearable I attempted to release some gas to relieve some of the pressure, but what I felt was more than just relief. I couldn't hold it back any longer. The inevitable happened, and I felt like I had grown five inches off my seat. What should I do? Where do I go? I almost ran out of the classroom, but instead, I just froze and began to pray that no one would notice the terrible stench which slowly wafted. It must have been close to 11:00 a.m., because some other kid raised his hand and asked to go to the bathroom, and lo and behold, the teacher let him go.

"God help me!" as I began praying more fervently. Now I had to wait for him to return. I waited about a minute and then quickly shot my hand up. Practically begging I asked if I could go. She said I had to wait. Urgently picked up my volume, and informed Mrs. Hoffman that I had been waiting since nine o'clock. "Is it an emergency?" she asked. I abruptly nodded, as she replied, "Go!" I don't know if anyone had gotten a whiff as I shot by. I didn't dare look back to see if anybody was holding their nose. As I rushed through the hallway, holding my backside now creamed with excrement, a little piece rolled down out of my pant leg onto the floor. I just couldn't leave any incriminating evidence behind, so I bent down to pick it up, and as I did, I was literally caught dirty handed. Standing by the bathroom door, was one of my new classmates. I will never forget the fear on Luis's face, as he launched into a quick stride looking back at me, as if afraid I might decide to throw the turd at him. I ran into the bathroom to clean

Reluctantly returning to the scene of the crime, I entered the classroom, keeping my eyes focused on the floor, to avoid looking directly at anyone, especially Luis. Mrs. Hoffman must have picked up the scent of my soiled stained pants as I quickly passed by her desk because she stopped me dead in my tracks. "Nelson," she sternly called after me. "Come here!" As I slowly turned to her, I felt my life's blood drain out of my face. It must have shown because she immediately replied, "You don't look very well, Nelson." As I approached her desk, everything inside me began to shake uncontrollably, and I feared that I would crap my pants again. The teacher looked intently into my face and proceeded to ask me the hardest question I would ever have to answer in school. "Did you do kaki on yourself?" She whispered. I could have died, but all I could do was look down in shame. Laughter, mocking, and shouts of "Pee-YEW!" followed close behind, as Mrs. Hoffman led me out of the classroom, down the hallway, and into the main office. Soon my mom was notified. As I sat there, I tried not to squirm to limit the unpleasant odor escaping the seat of my pants. I guess my efforts were futile, for although the office staff seemed very sympathetic, I could still notice some of them discreetly holding their breaths, while others just completely kept their distance.

Mama was right! It was a day I will never forget.

Rule 3: Don't Talk

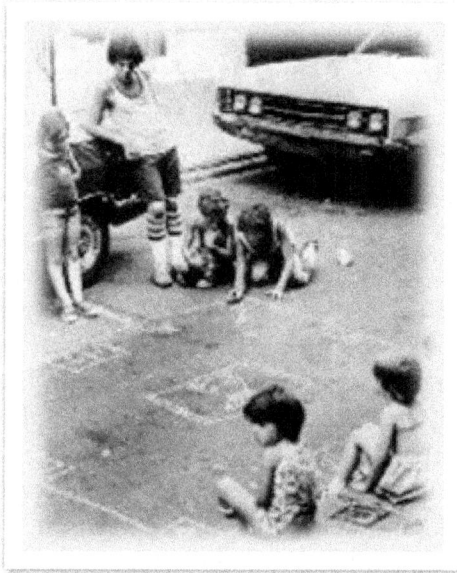

By the second grade, going to the bathroom became the most important part of my morning routine. I would wake up before my mom to be sure my bowels were clear so I could adhere to the 11 am rule. To be honest, I don't think Miss Hertzfeld really cared as much as I did, so my precautions were probably unmerited. The only thing she took very seriously was her prefix. I would call her Mrs., not knowing that I was assuming she was married. One day she barks back "It's Miss Hertzfeld." Looking back now, she must have been bitter about her situation. Miss or Mrs. Hertzfeld, I really didn't care.

She was a tall bony white woman, whose paleness reminded me of Morticia from the Addams Family. Although she lacked the subtle beauty of Carolyn Jones. Maybe that's why she wasn't married. In truth, our class might have been better if she had learned to be a bit more like Mrs. Hoffman. You could see her red face standing at the front of the class yelling "be quiet!"

NELSON COLÓN

I never saw Mrs. Hoffman's face change color. Most of the kids spoke whenever they felt like it. Sometimes they would talk about classwork, but most of the time their conversations would range from Gigantor the Space Age Robot, Astroboy to Skelzies. When the class volume exceeded that of the teacher, Miss Hertzfeld yelled with little effect on us. Despite this, I remembered my mother's rule and refrained from contributing to their conversations but listened intently.

I befriended a box at the rear of the class with three letters pasted on its side: SRA. It contained at least a hundred small booklets with all types of stories and topics. I started with the green ones because they seemed the easiest; stories by Dr. Seuss, Disney cartoon characters like Mickey Mouse, and Charles Shulz's Charlie Brown. Soon I was reading about adventurous characters like Don Quixote, King Arthur, The Three Musketeers, and the Count of Monte Cristo. Finally, I read through the red level and knew everything there was to know about Christopher Columbus, Paul Revere, and Martin Luther King Jr, or so I thought at the time. I liked reading it because it helped me adhere to rule three. After each booklet I would run to the teacher to tell her I finished, expecting her to reward me but all she would say was "Very Good Nelson." and pat me on the top of my head. I didn't like that but for some reason, I kept coming back to her for the same awkward reward. Though I wanted the teacher's praise, it was more important that I didn't receive any of my peers' disapproving glares. As a result, I rarely raised my hand. No one likes a Know-it-All. Also, It was a general rule that when you let the teacher know you had something to say, they always asked you to say more. I would much rather be able to return to my thoughts, avoiding eye contact with the teacher whenever she questioned us. Even chose to sit with the brighter kids, so I would be free to drift away from the classroom. Go back to my city in the clouds playing basketball with milk duds that melted in my hands before I could dunk them. I would run, run, and keep on running down off the clouds just in time to see Spot, Dick, and Jane run. Running so fast, passing through walls, beating every one of Speed Racer's track records. The crowds would cheer me on as I would pass through time to chase T-Rexes over steep cliffs, much like the Great Plains Native Indians did with the buffalo.

TRANSITION

At 8 years of age, I didn't understand the whole girl thing, how they made knees weak, or mouths mute but, little did I know, I was soon to find out. My sister Vero, short for Veronica, took me one Saturday afternoon to some girl's 8th birthday by the name of Georgina, whose nickname was like the hit song that was out during that time "Georgie Girl." The only dance I knew to do with Georgie was the Twist, immediately having my first puppy love experience. My sister Vero always took care of me and usually would take me wherever she went, also spoiling me and my brother Cano, with her own homemade version of Ring Dings, (chocolate mini-cakes) that she would make special for us on her EZ-Bake-Oven.

Rule 4: Be Kind

In third grade, I experienced my first crush. She was beautiful. She and I would talk all day long. I loved watching her work; she had this way of holding a pencil. She was always so organized and had this unquestioned confidence that was magnetic; drew the attention of those around her. She was Miss Herman, my third-grade teacher.

I quickly got her attention, raising my hand and volunteering for all the tasks. My enthusiasm quickly earned me the title of teacher's pet. She would greet me each morning with a smile and ask me, "How's my little daydreamer today?" Her voice would fish me out of the clouds as I often gazed out the window to watch pigeons perched on the awning of the bodega on the corner of Kosciuszko and Bushwick. The contrast of their faded gray and white feathers with the bright

35

yellow and red Grocery sign made it hard not to notice them. I often wondered what they were talking about, huddled in a similar fashion to the men beneath them. Together as if an NFL team is ready to compete with some invisible opponent? A group of men huddled beneath them all day long, talking, laughing, stumbling, and selling something that wasn't available in the store. I wondered if they plotted who they would aim for next. "Nelson?", "Huh...Yes, Teacher?" "Where were you just now?" "I'm sorry Miss Herman... I don't know... where would you like me to be?" As the year progressed, my lack of focus earned me fewer endearing nicknames from my peers: Along with daydreamer, came sleepyhead, slowpoke, and even an occasional "stupid!" Even Miss Herman took to the name sleepy head. But it was different when she used it because she attached a few explicit words, "Nelson, my little sleepy head."

Just before Thanksgiving, we cut out some turkey feathers and pasted them to 99-cent disposable plates. My mother loved these keepsakes; she would proudly display them on the refrigerator with various fruit magnets. I might have gone a little overboard with the glue, so I had to get more. Anyway, I knew it would allow me another opportunity to catch a glimpse of my future wife. She was on the way, as I approached her I formed a smile, trying not to show too many teeth to seem creepy. She put her leg out as if she intended to trip me. I smiled harder and changed course to pass her by, still maintaining eye contact to get a closer look at her sapphire gaze. Suddenly, I felt myself falling, right into her wooden chair, knocking a few scraps of orange, yellow, and brown construction paper off her desk. Aside from my self-confidence shattering, I could hear Miss Herman yelp, "You tore my stocking! Nelson, you tore my stocking!" My peers started to laugh. From the unevenly waxed floor, I looked up at Miss Herman expecting her to save me from any further embarrassment, but the implausible happened. She smiled. She had tripped me on purpose. Finishing a soft chuckle, Miss Herman said, "Nelson, you need to watch where you are going... I put my leg out, but I thought you saw it. You must pay more attention to where you are going. You can't live your life with your head in the clouds." She tripped me on purpose! Still fallen, she continued her monologue, "I can't believe you tore my stocking?" She chuckled, "I can't believe you didn't see my leg." The volume of her voice receded as I wondered, 'Why would a teacher want me to fall? Why isn't she helping me up? Is she laughing at me too?' It was then that Miss Herman's eyes glowed in a different way, less like the witch of the north and more like the wicked witch of the south. I helped myself up to my feet. It took what seemed like a lifetime as I tried to remember what my mother had told me; about *Rule 4: **To Be Kind**.*

"I'm sorry Miss Herman", my voice cracked as I tried to swallow my tears." She didn't respond, but instead turned around to resume helping students who were still stumbling on their laughter, conveying "you're so stupid" stares. "That wasn't very kind," I thought.

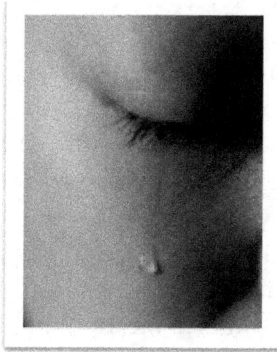

Rule 5: Pay Attention

Trying to pay attention to Miss Herman was like holding on to the damp railing of a crow's nest through the eyewall of a storm, gripping harder with every passing second, unsure if the next wind would toss me into the unknown. If I were aboard a pirate ship amidst a storm, I would allow my body to flail back and forth, swallow the pain the rain inflicted on my chest, and allow my legs to lift high into the heavens, so that my grip would be the only thing keeping me alive. I might even let go, especially if there were a Kraken. I would want to see where those tentacles would take me; some underwater cavern with thousands of bioluminescent creatures never seen by a human eye before. Or maybe, before I was consumed, I would be snatched up by what seemed to be a mermaid but turned out to be sirens, clawing at my legs and stomach as I fought my way out of their clutches with my rusty cutlass. "Nelson, Nelson!" "Huh?" I would murmur, as my name would resuscitate me. The class was filled with familiar chuckles. "Yes, Miss Herman," I finally responded. "Who have you chosen for your project?"

At this point, the only thing I had in common with Miss Herman was that we both grew increasingly excited as the year drew closer to an end. For me, it was the summer vacation, but for her, it was a research project she talked about since September. All year, she would hang it over our heads. Oh yes, this could be something you could use in your project, make sure you use titles, headings, and one of these new vocabulary words, also don't forget to use complete sentences, and a variety of other nonsense. Now we had to choose a historically famous American, write a whole two pages, and stand in front of the class to read it aloud. Everyone hated reading aloud, except that prissy little know-it-all Priscilla. Miss Herman wouldn't allow anyone to do Martin Luther King Jr., because she deemed it "inappropriate." News of his assassination earlier that month made it an extraordinarily sensitive topic. I guess it raised too many questions she didn't feel equipped to answer as a white woman. Are we safe? Are we next? Is it because he's black? Why don't people like Black people? Isn't it right to fight for equality? Are they targeting Latinos next? "Martin Luther King," I said with confidence. "Nelson, I said we are not doing Martin Luther King." "Huh... Oh, I didn't know... who can I do?"

TRANSITION

As Miss Herman started down a list of "acceptable" historic figures, the names **George Washington and Abraham Lincoln** jumped out at me because I saw them on some weird white mountain and discarded couch coins at home. I wondered who would win if they battled it out. I mean, Abe was a giant compared to G Wash. School was chock-full of rhymes and songs that portrayed him as an ax-wielding tough guy who wouldn't let anyone get in the way of him achieving whatever he set his mind to. Yeah, G Wash beat a supposedly unbeatable foe in the British Navy, but he didn't do it alone, he had his **X-Men,** * Franklin, Hamilton, Adams, and Jefferson. The guy had a dream team fighting alongside him to win his fights. Anyway, in most of the paintings and pictures I see of him, he's wearing this lame wig and doing none of the hard work, like rowing the boat. It almost seemed like he thought he was too good to roll up his sleeves and get things done. **Abe, on the other hand, got dirty**; used his supreme intelligence and strategy to pummel all the southern states into submission. It doesn't matter if they were better fighters, better trained, or a better shot with a rifle, he wore them down and won. In that way, he was both Bruce Banner's brains and the Hulk's brawn. Abe wouldn't even need to lay a hand on G Wash; he would cower in his presence, scared one good hulk smash would do him in. Then again, G Wash's track record suggested that he wouldn't back down even if outmatched. G Wash led the U.S. to victory against a seemingly unbeatable British fleet. The man killed hundreds as a soldier and thousands as a General. Abe doesn't have those numbers. That sword G Wash always sported in old paintings and photos seemed better than Abe's stupid ax. But he probably didn't need his sword to put Lincoln down. Matter of fact, G Wash was a straight-up assassin. Didn't he assassinate some guy which pretty much started the whole French Indian War in the first place? The dude starts wars and ends them. In any case, assassins are Lincoln's weak spot, we all know that. If John Wilkes Booth could get him while he was watching some play, then I'm sure G Wash could have gotten it done. Then again, G Wash surrendered at Fort Necessity.

The Hulk would never... I felt the weight of everyone's eyes on me; something was wrong. Everyone's looking at me, including Miss Herman, "Nelson?" Her high pitch let me know it was a question. "Huh, What?" I glanced at Priscilla to see her reaction, and the smile on her face told me that Miss Herman had just asked me a question. Do I make something up or do I fess up? "It's okay my little sleepyhead," I didn't like when she called me that anymore. "Who will you choose?" She insisted on a response. "I'm sorry Miss Herman, I wasn't paying attention."

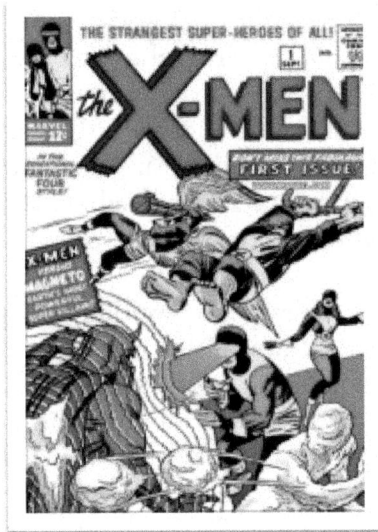

X-Men MARVEL Comic was launched in 1963 by Stan Lee and Jack Kirby

Rule 6: Don't Run

As 3rd grade approached its end, I turned nine. My best birthday gift was the latest news. Mom smiled as she announced "Los estamos moviendo."[20] We got our own place. It was a small two-bedroom, on the second floor of a three-story apartment building. It wasn't very far from Titi's three-story two-family house—just beyond the redline that separated the two districts. This was the end of having to live on Titi Gladys' immense patience. She was sad to see us go, but mom celebrated the opportunity of having her own place; kept on saying something about needing privacy.

As a result, we spent most of the summer lugging boxes one at a time into my uncle's yellow Chevy. There was cause for excitement about our new place, but it wasn't the initial focus of my attention. While my family was busy moving in, I ran to a tenement across the street. I had never seen anything like it; the cracks in the brick and the color of the dated mortar. Out of the twenty huge checkerboard windows viewable from the curb, only six weren't boarded up and tagged with fluorescent orange Xs. I wondered what memories it held, more pleasant or painful. I felt happy when I noticed the top-floor windows were still intact. It was probably because they were too high to toss a rock through, but I chose to believe it to be a sign of life; the tenement refusing to die; a survivor of sorts. I was curious about its

41

story, but it remained silent. We had smaller, suitcase-sized windows in our new home. Many were even protected, probably so we would not befall the same boarded-up fate of the tenement across the street. Thick iron bars guarded the first-floor windows against passersby that wanted to prove their good aim to their friends.

Thankfully our second-story windows weren't barred, giving my mother the freedom to stick her head out into the street and locate me whenever she wanted. It was a small railroad apartment; through the kitchen, you could immediately see what would be my mother's bedroom which she would share with me. The next adjoining room became my sister Veronica's, flowing out into the living room where my big bro Cano would reside on mom's gold and clear plastic upholstered couch. This is a source of some funny eventful memories for us, but deep-rooted resentment for my brother to this day. He still talks of being tortured by the sound and the feel of plastic-covered couch cushions, and how he couldn't sleep past sunrise because it was too painful; the ultra-heated layer of plastic literally ripping his skin red. I couldn't help but smile when he almost lost an entire eyebrow because his pillow went missing in his sleepy shuffle.

My sister Lilly might have shared my brother's fate, but at this point she was out, married, pregnant with my first nephew, and living only a short walk away on the borderline of Bushwick-Ridgewood. It appeared that our mom rarely slept in her room, most nights waging a futile war against the apartment, cleaning well into tomorrow and passing out on the Formica kitchen table. I wondered if she missed Papi[21] or if she felt relieved to be free of him, or both. Back then I was glad to get the queen-size mattress all to myself, but now I wonder if I was a reminder of what she was running from. Did I remind her of him? Do I look too much like him? When she saw me asleep, was she struck with the fear that once gripped her in our lime-green house in Puerto Rico?

TRANSITION

The roaches and mice lived there long before us; plugging every hole she could find with steel wool was a valiant but vain attempt by my mother. I felt the safest from their intrusion while in the bathroom or kitchen because the walls were clothed with green clovers and yellow flowers; the wallpaper peeled away where it met the ceiling and bubbled by the stove but appeared the smoothest in the bathroom. As a result, the bathroom became my haven, but even that eventually changed, claiming my security as its first casualty of war. A patch of wallpaper came down onto my back as I was sitting on the toilet. At first, I didn't think much of it until I felt their invasion marching on the back of my neck and on my thighs. German Nazi roaches infiltrated me. I ran out into the kitchen with my pants dragged by my ankles, my mother was not sure whether she should scold or hold me until she spotted the egg larvae in my hair. From that day on I solely trusted the walls in the sala.[22] They were older than me, but sad, resembling crying faces, tears forming from the ceiling to the floorboard. Later, my brother told me it was just a bad paint job, "The walls don't have any feeling" Cano corrected, "the super probably got some guy off the street to just throw some paint on them." In contrast, the ceiling seemed as if it was in a continual state of celebration, decorated with ornate tin patches. The only thing that got a fresh coat of silver paint every year was the cast iron heater, while everything around it grew older and more yellow. Maybe it was because it complained loudly, always whistling, clanging, and chipping layers of paint onto the floor.

NELSON COLÓN

September 1967

Bushwick Avenue was nowhere as 'Ghetto' as Bleecker St. Entering 4th Grade. I was zoned to P.S. 75. Despite the school's proximity to our new home, I had to wake up early so I wouldn't be late for my first day entering fourth grade. She combed my hair, filled my belly, and made sure I left on time. She had to leave for work simultaneously and was adamant about us walking at least part of the way together. As I waited for my mom to get ready, I sat on the front stoop with my burgundy briefcase on my lap; a relic my mother had fished out of a local thrift shop. It was the oldest thing I had ever seen, the brass edges dented, and rusted red. I would only close one of the latches because they got stuck if you closed both. The leather handle had several cracks which could've cut my palm like a razor if I weren't careful. Its contents were an egg and cheese sandwich wrapped in a brown paper bag, three pencils, and a notebook with half the pages ripped out. I had recycled it from the year before, throwing last year's notes and handouts into a dresser drawer as if I would refer to them at some point in the future.

"Vámonos, vámonos!"[23] mom yelled as she nearly shoved me off the front stoop. Yanking my arm behind her, moving faster than my legs could carry me she said, "You can't be late." The school was about 15 minutes away, but I'd have to make it in ten. The fact her gaze was three blocks ahead told me our goodbye would be brief. We parted ways on Bleecker and Evergreen, hurriedly howling "Don't Run," knowing full well I'd have to. On the way to school, the sounds of car wheels crashing into potholes as they whizzed by, fire engine sirens

44

blaring, and the incessant honking of gypsy cabs trying to compete for pick-ups made it hard for me to refrain from spectating. When I realized I was watching my surroundings more than making progress, I started to skip every other step telling myself "This isn't running. Mom said no running, right?"

My first day at P.S. 75 was uneventful, full of the usual moments of awkwardness as each of us had to stand and share our summer happenings. But as the year dragged on, school became increasingly treacherous. It wasn't long before I realized I might as well have painted a massive bullseye on the back of my head. My chubby appearance, coupled with my mom's insistence on me lugging around a colossal, painfully "uncool" briefcase, made me an easy target for Frankie Pepitone—a big blonde-haired Italian boy. He didn't like it when I didn't have a nickel or dime to fork over. One inopportune time, outside the boy's bathroom, he overpowered me and pinned me against the wall. I started to cry as he rummaged through my pockets, declaring "Anything I find I keep?" as if he were asking me permission; like I could answer anything other than, "Sure you can!" I remembered, for a moment, the boy on the red bike. I needed to be free of him, so I used the only weapon I had at my disposal; wailing the burgundy briefcase repeatedly, hoping the rusted metal tips would hit him in the face. Unfortunately, all I did was strike his wrist once, which only made him more determined to hurt me. I took my briefcase in two hands in one last desperate attempt to hurl it at him, but he yanked it away from me before I could finish launching it. He threw it down and stomped on the briefcase until his foot went straight through. "Nooo" I wailed, as my knees suddenly buckled, and the wind knocked right out of me with a left hook to the ribs. Frankie and his bully cohorts ran off when our home teacher Miss Bolduc approached us yelling "Cut it out!"

My mom had to pick me up that day, but I never told anyone what happened, after all, "snitches get stitches." It wasn't one of my mother's rules, but it seemed just as valid. Freddy Marquez always used to say, "snitches get stitches." He was short sporting a shag cut and wore bell bottoms. He quickly became known as the "Hippy Puerto Rican" and liked the same girl I liked. A petit tom-boyish blonde girl by the name of Jean. We became friends almost immediately because we were the same kindred spirits, admiring a girl from afar, too nervous, and ashamed to admit it to each other.

My Mom took me and my newfound sidekick to the Broadway Loew's to see a musical based on a love story between a young Italian man who falls in love with a beautiful Puerto Rican girl. Although it was the first musical we had ever seen, we were mesmerized by the singing and dancing and yet cool storyline. The plot takes place on the upper West side of Manhattan and rather accurately portrays the tense relations of Puerto Ricans, Italians, and Irish immigrants who were crowded into a heavily occupied ghetto neighborhood. The turf was being run by an Italian gang, and as the Puerto Rican minority started moving into the neighborhood, the Hispanic youth began experiencing confrontations. This united them as they sought strength in numbers, forming their own gang. As they ready for a rumble, they show the Italian gang marching together swinging their chains while simultaneously switching to show the other side of the tracks... The Puerto Rican gang arming themselves with their knives and clubs, while both gangs began singing. *

TRANSITION

*****West Side Story**: *a 1961 American musical[1] romantic drama[2] film directed by Robert Wise[3] and Jerome Robbins[4]. With a screenplay by Ernest Lehman[5], the film is an adaptation of the 1957 Broadway musical of the same title[6] which in turn was inspired by Shakespeare[7]'s play Romeo and Juliet[8]*

It was really exhilarating to watch. Freddy and I came out of the movie dancing and singing to the rumbling tune all the way back home, while my mom just found us amusing. Freddy and I became so inspired by the movie, we started to save our lunch money to purchase a couple of folding pocketknives. We imagined that it would help us ward off two Puerto Rican gangster wannabes that had arisen in the ranks. Felix and his brother who everyone called "Monkey."

---

1. https://en.wikipedia.org/wiki/Musical_film

2. https://en.wikipedia.org/wiki/Romantic_drama

3. https://en.wikipedia.org/wiki/Robert_Wise

4. https://en.wikipedia.org/wiki/Jerome_Robbins

5. https://en.wikipedia.org/wiki/Ernest_Lehman

6. https://en.wikipedia.org/wiki/West_Side_Story

7. https://en.wikipedia.org/wiki/William_Shakespeare

8. https://en.wikipedia.org/wiki/Romeo_and_Juliet

To this day I don't know his real name. Everyone branded him "Monkey" because he resembled a scary hairy monkey. I don't know if it was this that fueled his chronically angry demeanor or the fact that he lived on a bench in the local park. I assumed he liked it because his brother used his nickname regularly. They were older, high school dropouts who were infamous in our neighborhood for ripping off young grade-schoolers like us. Usually, they were accompanied by their scout Tony, aka "lil Tone," a loyal runt about our age that Monkey and Felix had inducted into their crew, often terrorizing us for our lunch money in the mornings. Freddy was a lot more clever than I was, concocting better hiding places for his money than I did. On our way home one day he lit up, "I got it!" I got enough for both of us." I didn't know what he meant. I thought it couldn't be the money for the knives because we were consistently robbed of our lunch money almost every day.

Almost in response to that, he reached into his underwear and pulled out over five dollars in quarters, dimes, and nickels, wrapped in tin foil. Freddy took one for the team. Before you knew it, we had our sleek brand-new K55s, quickly opening and closing them while acting out the parts we liked best in West Side Story. I sang, "We're gonna hand 'em a surprise." Freddy responded, "We're gonna cut 'em down to size." With that, ironically enough, that lil demon Tony came out of nowhere taking us off guard, as he snuck up behind us, "What's that, what you guys got there?" I turned to him and said, "What's it to you?" holding up the open knife and cutting it through the air in his direction. Fear struck Tony's brow slightly. Freddy realized what I was doing and followed up with, "Yeah, back up runt before we cut you!" Tony's face never did arrive at fear, instead, it shifted from confusion to excitement. "Oh yeah, so you guys think you bad now, huh?" he retorted to our newfound courage, as he ran across the street and down an alleyway. Panic instantly struck Freddy as he grabbed me, "Why'd you do that?" "What you mean man? You're the one who said you're gonna cut him." "But you're the one who..." Before Freddy could make his point, his eyes were set on the alleyway in which lil Tone had disappeared just a minute ago. Out came Monkey and Felix, cars screeching and halting mere inches from their sides as they ran through traffic, making a beeline toward us.

Until that moment, the short-lived courage we mustered up went right out the window, as we wanted nothing more than to run. God knows that we tried to evade them dozens of times before, and even got away on rare occasions, but my mother's warning rang through my head like a blaring siren, "Don't run" as I looked down at the knife in my hand. I don't have to run," I thought. "I can stand and fight," I gripped the knife hard and drew it back lower by my waist, bending my knees, at the ready. Suddenly, breathing became more difficult. Maybe because I realized we weren't in a musical; Monkey wouldn't merely just dodge out of the way as if choreographed. Maybe I couldn't breathe because I was afraid that I might cut him, hurt him, kill him even, God forbid. Or maybe it was because both of his hands were already around my neck before I could even react.

Honestly, I don't recall exactly. What I do remember is being hoisted off the ground and colliding with a brick wall that was sharper than I would have expected. I could feel it cutting into my back as I was forced to eat his filthy breath; that is when his grip would allow me a breath of soiled air. Monkey was the bum; it was well-known that he lived on a bench in Knickerbocker Park. His wild nasty hair was unkempt, and pieces of grass, glass, and bird dropping littered what he thought was a fro but was more of a mountain range of tangled knots. Felix was clean and in turn more popular with the ladies in the neighborhood. When he wasn't with his brother, he usually sported some young girl on his arm even though he reeked of cheap cologne. He lived above the hardware store down the street, greased his hair, and wore a small fedora-style black beaver brim, with a blue feather as if he thought himself a goodfella.

They were too quick; disarming us before we could react. Lil' Tony picked up our K55s where we had dropped them, pleased at the power he possessed. My panic wouldn't allow me to cry, only claw at Monkey's hands. He let go with one hand and set me on my feet. I was relieved that I could now feel the ground beneath me, at least to the extent of allowing me to tippy toe on my now raggedy PF Flyers. I couldn't see Freddy, but somehow, I knew the look in Felix's eyes was now more important, his stare fixed on Monkey, as if afraid, "Monkey, don't do it!" Monkey had pulled out a meat hook and pressed it against my jugular. He fixated on the spot where it met my skin, a savage look in his eyes, his head weaving side to side as if a cobra ready to strike.

I wondered if I deserved this, if my mother would be upset with me for not coming straight home. If I would end up bleeding out on the street, or at least making it to a hospital so I could say goodbye. Monkey didn't cut me. He took his anger out on the wall behind me, sparks from the hook clashing with the bricks and mortar almost lit Monkey's mangled hair on fire. They threw us to the ground laughing a wild hysterical cackle as they walked off with their reward, our fear, and our knives.

Naturally, getting picked on regularly, coupled with my lack of athleticism, meant I would never successfully fight off the bullies that accompanied or came after Felix and Monkey. But at least I wouldn't run too far. Most of the time, running would earn me a trip to the pavement and a taste of fresh blood. Over time, I learned that staring them down could ward off the less determined. Changing my route home to intentionally pass my Bodega on Menahan & Central Avenue helped too. I would feel a sense of relief when I would spot the "neighborhood watch," a slew of local pot dealers standing outside the Deli-Dinette Soda Fountain Shoppe. If I had the money I would go in and sit on a stool at the mini-soda fountain area. They would hook me up with a slamming egg cream. If I had an extra 35 cents in my pocket, I'd be sure to also pick up an RC Cola and a Jolly Rancher Stick.

On my way out I would feel an unshakable inclination to run or at the least rush past the smoking men outside. Instead, I would make sure to pay homage because no one wants to be a victim of a home invasion when they are away from home. I looked one in the eyes and said, "High guys," as I waved. "Hey, little man... Nice briefcase," they replied cordially, not catching the meaning of my pun. "See you later," I would say while hoping that wasn't the case. Their nonchalant, purposeless demeanor made me fearful because I knew from experience boredom is a dangerous motivator. Grandma always said, *"idle hands are the devil's workshop"*[24] Slowly as I passed them, I remembered my mother's words, **"Don't Run."**

Rule 7: Do Your Best

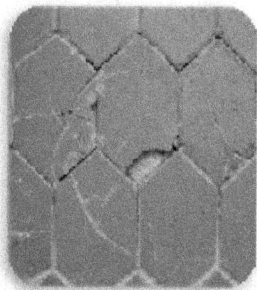

During my last year, I began feeling safe within the walls of my school, so to say that I loved to walk the halls of P.S. 75 was an understatement. I really enjoyed examining the light gleam off the waxed floors, especially the sporadic patterns formed by the warped and cracked tiles; a consequence of decades of small feet traversing the floors and halls. The tiles that ran along the corner of the wall were black, while the reddish-brown tiles ran down the middle of the hall like an ancient red carpet. I assume the corners tiles were purposefully black because the corners were always the hardest to clean, so why try? The corner outside my sixth-grade classroom had the most interesting cracks. If I were not careful, I would spend well over my five-minute minimum staring at the patterns; my teacher's head poking out the classroom door echoing my name down the hall. The bathroom pass was my partner, keeping me company on my long walks. The windows littered the top of the classroom doors and allowed a look at the ceiling of every classroom. What was the point? Did anyone ever peer in through those windows? If they were meant as a means of escape in the case of an emergency, why were they reinforced, inlaid with steel wire situated in diamond-shaped patterns?

There wasn't much point in being in class anyway. In sixth grade, to compensate for my lack of athletic ability, I concentrated on my studies and became an honor student. Earning a string of A's inspired the bullies to add "geek" and "nerd" to the labels they already hurled at me. I would find solace in a box of independent reading booklets collecting dust at the back of the classroom. Ms. Simone was content with me missing her lessons because she knew I was tired of going over the multiplication table. I benefited more from reading excerpts from Steinbeck and Twain's novels examining the historical context of Revere, Lincoln, and Martin Luther King Jr. My homeroom teacher Mr. Abrams wasn't teaching much of anything new at this point of the year.

Except for this one morning when he introduced us to the *Evelyn Wood Speed Reading Course*. **Evelyn Nielsen Wood** (January 8, 1909 – August 26, 1995) was an American educator. She created and marketed a system said to increase a reader's speed (over the average reading rate of 250 to 300 words a minute) by a factor of three to ten times or more, while preserving and even improving comprehension.

Mr. Abrams was curious to see if it truly worked and if it could help us not only read the assigned books faster but also improve our comprehension. Lo and behold, we found that our reading speed did increase significantly, and we understood the content up to 25 percent better. I still practice the concept to this day. Has a way of really helping me stay more focused on what I'm reading, as well as with my writing. Thank you, Mr. Abrams!

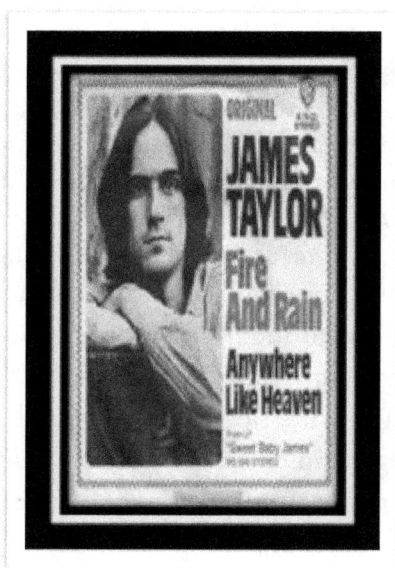

All the classrooms at my end of the 3rd floor were obsessed with preparing for the sixth-grade graduation. The entire graduating class was required to memorize and sing Fire & Rain* by James Taylor.[25] All the classrooms practiced in the mornings in preparation for afternoon assembly. I would sing along during my frequent trips to the bathroom as the lyrics rang through the hallway. In the '60s, the British Invasion introduced the Beatles. You were either a Beatles fan[9] or an Elvis man[10]. I was leaning more toward the King of Rock & Roll. Come 1969 a fresh new group came out of the shadows of Gary, Indiana: The Jackson Five[11] discovered by Diana Ross[12]; launched their first hit with Motown[13], "I Want You Back[14]."

---

9. https://www.youtube.com/watch?v=jenWdylTtzs

10. https://www.youtube.com/watch?v=MfrC8PAQtlg

11. https://www.youtube.com/watch?v=c0rGI-Pkmtk&t=228s

12. https://www.youtube.com/watch?v=d3DqntnXSZ0

13. https://www.youtube.com/watch?v=byZ_9W_3jOc

14. https://www.youtube.com/watch?v=y2bVIBwpCTA

"Fire and Rain" is a folk-rock song. After its release, "Fire and Rain" peaked at number two on RPM's Canada Top Singles chart and at number three on the Billboard Hot 100. The second line "Suzanne the plans they made put an end to you" refers to Suzanne Schnerr, a childhood friend of his who died by suicide. Taylor completed writing the song while in rehab[15]. In 2005, during an interview on NPR[16], Taylor explained to host Scott Simon[17] that the song was written in three parts: The second part details Taylor's struggle to overcome drug addiction and depression.

Most of my classmates would complain when they lined us up for our daily trip to the auditorium, but I loved to sing. I still do. Music has a way of lifting me out of my body to a place where I feel free. I believe music is a mere expression of our inner soul, so why not play on? The first time I sang in unison with the entire student body was, dare I say, a spiritual experience. As a matter of fact, James Taylor was the first person who taught me about Jesus.

*"Won't you look down upon me, **Jesus** You've got to help me make a stand! You've just got to see me through another day."* Got me thinking about Heaven. If it were real? If **He** were real? James Taylor called out to Jesus Christ for help, that he would help him endure another day, and alleviate his pain. I remember hearing distinctly about a Jesus movement around that same time, where many "hippies" were flocking to the West Coast and getting baptized in the bay areas of southern California. *

The Jesus revival movement, also known as the Jesus revolution, began in the late 1960s and early 1970s, particularly in the United States. It was a spiritual awakening and cultural phenomenon characterized by a renewed interest in Jesus Christ and the teachings of the Bible, predominantly among the young people of that era.

15. https://en.wikipedia.org/wiki/Drug_rehabilitation
16. https://en.wikipedia.org/wiki/National_Public_Radio
17. https://en.wikipedia.org/wiki/Scott_Simon

TRANSITION

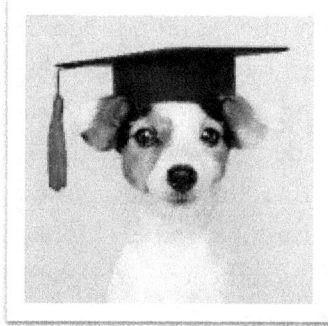

When you are from Bushwick, you enter a paradoxical relationship with pride and pain. The things that cause you the most pain, and seek to destroy you, are the things you inevitably resent and blame. Yet, struggle and strife become the very things which ultimately make you stronger, hardens you, makes you tough, refines you into a man. Being from the ghetto was itself a necessary marriage of victory and vice.

On the day of graduation, Mrs. Glass issued an idle threat every few minutes before our final performance, "if you don't get this right you're not graduating!" I think we all knew she couldn't see her threat through, but we were fearful just the same. We were required to hold hands during the song, and my line partner was this cute slender girl with long black shiny hair and piercing green eyes named Yvonne. So, I was more than happy to oblige every time. During every practice, I especially liked that she would take my hand before I built up the courage to take hers. Miss Nugent waved her arms like a madwoman every time we were off-key or singing at different paces. She would restart the metronome situated next to a microphone and it would begin again, but not today. Today we had only one shot, and she already forewarned, she wouldn't restart us or point out how badly we were singing. She had to maintain her composure for the principal and parents.

Most of us sang the lyrics directly from the piece of paper they handed out to us more than a month ago. I lost the lyrics the first day they gave them out, but no one knew because I had memorized the song that first night, singing myself to sleep, driving my brother Cano crazy as I serenaded him well until midnight. Today, the song finished more quickly than I usually did, or maybe it seemed that way because we only went through it once. I looked for my mother in the crowd of parents that lined the left and right sides of the overcrowded auditorium. I knew she would be standing because she couldn't get off work early, and most likely would be arriving late.

They began handing out the "Graduation" certificates and had each of us walk across the stage, as Principal Martinez addressed us. He took the blood straight out of my face when I heard my name being called first. "Nelson Colón, we would like to present you with the Principal Award for completing the most Strategic and Independent Reading Assignments in the city of New York. Congratulations!" I also received an award for having taken first place in the 6th Grade Spelling Bee earlier that semester. It turned out that the dusty box of reading packets at the back of Ms. Simone's class was worth my while. I climbed the creaky step of the stage to shake Principal Martinez's hand and caught Freddy's ecstatic smile from afar. Freddy, who was a lot more gifted in music and the arts, was awarded a Certificate acknowledging him as the "Top Artist" of our Graduating Class.

As my mother surprised me at the bottom of the steps, nearly lifting me off the ground with a hug. I heard the words I didn't realize I had yearned to hear forever. "**Mijo** [26], I'm so proud of you!" Teary-eyed, I repeated to her the 7th and most sacred golden rule: *"It's all because of you Ma, that ..."*

I will always do my best!"

Chapter Four

Black Mass

Approaching the age of 11, as a "good" Catholic, I was expected to get ready for my first holy communion. To my mother, it was a rite of passage. She sat me down, inspected me from head to toe, combed her fingers through my hair, brushed dandruff from my shoulders, and the poor condition of my sneakers, my laces tattered at the edges because I would rather tuck than tie them. She said, "Son, you'll be a man soon. Do you know what that means?" She looked at me as if a bit sad. For a moment, I thought she might be sending me away and I immediately feared I wouldn't have time to pack my nine-inch TV. Saturday mornings wouldn't be the same without Jonny Quest, Space Ghost, and Bugs Bunny. Not to mention, the sound and sight of my mother persistently stirring cornmeal on the stove. Is she saying goodbye? Would I ever see her again? She started to explain what it would be like to be a man. At first, I was skeptical of her words because she's, well, a woman. I wondered, how did she know what a man should be, or could be if she weren't one herself. What I know now is that the absence of my father gave her the insight most mothers didn't have. Looking back, she knew what a man shouldn't be more than what a man should. She listed the things to avoid rather than emulate in a tone more accusatory than I expected. Was I guilty of these things already? She listed "Don't be afraid, don't be weak, don't run from your problems, don't be disloyal, don't be abusive, don't be like your father." The list was long, but not quite as long as the golden rules for school, so I felt confident that I could check them off much like I did the last. In any case, I had already met most of the criteria.

That week, she picked me up from school early so we could make our way over to St. Barbara's, conveniently located across the street from where we lived. As we entered through the castle-like doors of the Cathedral, my mother tightly gripped my hand drawing me closer to her side, to discourage me from stopping at the archways. I was immobilized by them, wondering how tall they were. In our small apartment, I could leap and touch the ceiling, if I trampolined off my mother's plastic-covered sofas. If Cano were here, even with his height and superior athleticism, he would probably fail to reach the highest point of this dark gothic place.

I stared into the sculpted walls like a night sky and wondered if this was what heaven would look like, enamored at how artistic and ancient it was. I wondered what stories the walls held. We walked by some statues of people I didn't know. Everything seemed so orderly and important, too clean, too pretty. I reached out for one of the sculpted feet and was met with a swift slap to the back of my hand, "Don't touch that!" she said in a stern whisper. We came to a man lighting a stage of votive candles; his name was Father Gleason. When he shook my hand,

TRANSITION

I was taken by surprise at how sweaty his palms were. I looked at my mother, wondering if I could wipe my hand on my shirt. As soon as she looked away I did. He escorted us both to class where I was officially handed over to Sister Mary Hannah. The class had already commenced, and she seemed irritated about having to pause her lecture when we entered. I began to sweat as my mother conferenced with the priest and nun in Spanish.

I wasn't instructed to sit so I scanned the room for an empty seat. There were two in the front and a single empty desk in the back beside none other than my good friend Sigfredo, a.k.a. "Freddy." I knew his parents were Catholic too, but I didn't expect him to be there. It all made sense now, why he was absent from school that day. He was probably home all day being prepped and coached for his first day of Religious Instructions. My mother exited and the sister's subtle head nod told me I should find a seat. She stopped me as I headed for Sigfredo and asked me to sit in the front.

She resumed, mentioning the Eucharist, the crucifixion of Jesus Christ, and the significance of our first communion. I had no idea what she was talking about, but she spoke with such confidence that I found it reassuring. The last of my nervousness subsided, replaced by excitement. It was nice to think that God was interested in me. The thought that he cared about me sounded nice, but a bit impossible. After all, I'm one person out of billions. In any case, if he did love me, where was He when I was molested?

Suddenly, I realized Sister Mary Hannah's eyes were fixed on mine. Did I miss something? Did she ask me a question? "What is the Eucharist, Nelson?" she asked, slightly irritated. I was dead in the water. I was caught in my own head again. Before I could piece together a guess, an eager little girl said, "It's the blood and body of Christ!" almost jumping out of her seat. Blood and body of Christ? What had I gotten myself into? I remained silent as fear barged in. The Sister went on to say how it was the heart of "Christian initiation," but I thought it sounded rather cannibalistic.

"We eat him?" I blurted aloud, meaning to keep it to my inner debate. "Yes, and No," the sister said, further confusing me. She went on to explain, her irritated demeanor replaced by a seemingly genuine excitement. Her faith brought her a joy I rarely saw in others. Even though it all seemed rather violent and a bit scary she didn't seem to think so. Every word raised her spirit, making me want what she had.

The weeks and months pressed on, and these exchanges increased in both frequency and intensity. Did he die for me? Why? He didn't even know me. I didn't know if there was anyone, I loved so much that I would die for them; my cowardice would probably prevent me from even wanting to save my family. If this were the case, he was braver than anyone or anything I could fathom. What I realized was that dying for someone was the ultimate test of love and it was this love Jesus seemed to have for me. Did he love me? Still, love me? The love of God didn't seem possible because it wasn't contingent on someone loving him back. God came down from heaven to love, teach, heal, and try to change the corrupt hearts of people who didn't care to know him. Wow, what love! As a matter of fact, he tried his hardest to change the very people who sent him to his execution.

Religious Instructions were a great privilege. Not to mention, it didn't hurt that I was let out early, with Sigfredo, every Wednesday. While on the route, our conversations usually focused on the newly learned words we never knew existed, words like sin, soul, salvation, and damnation. We knew

what our hearts were, in our brain or our body, but this soul thing was a new curious concept. Was it in my heart? My mind? Did it run from my head to my toes or was it like a shadow, extending endlessly from my feet depending on how brightly the sun shone? Could I hurt it? Or was it both invincible and vulnerable? I would try to ask my mother some of these questions, but she wouldn't attempt to answer. She had delegated the responsibility of religion to others. Questions continued to be surmounted. Suddenly, the word soul was everywhere. I would hear it coming from the open doors of the record stores, a man not singing, but practically screaming, "I got SOUL and I'm Superbad!" Huh? Just didn't make any sense. How can having "soul" be a bad thing? Robert Johnson claimed to have had a soul but sold it to the devil like it was something we can bargain with. Existing with no body, Georgie and Casper were still friendly souls, helping others, all the while, unable to help themselves. And then there was "The Little Prince," * floating from planet to planet and befriending a stranded pilot. The fox's secret was eerily familiar to Sister Mary Hannah, *"It is only with the heart and one's soul that one can truly begin to see rightly:*

For what is essential is invisible to the eye. [27]

NELSON COLÓN

May 1969

After six months of instruction, I was ready for my first communion, or so I was told. Imagined God was watching me with deep admiration as I made my way down the aisle as if I were the Little Prince.

Coincidentally, a couple of months later, during the Apollo 11 mission, astronauts Neil Armstrong and Buzz Aldrin gracefully touched the lunar surface on that transcendent July 20, 1969. I felt a kinship with them somehow, as a profound connection stirred within me. Much like those intrepid astronauts landing on the illuminated face of the moon, I sensed a parallel journey which had taken place in my own life. It felt as though I, too, had traversed from the shadowy realms to the radiant embrace of the light.

As I drew closer to the altar, an unseen organist played, my mother waved from the pews, and I smiled hard enough that my cheeks almost cracked. Glancing over at the girl beside me, I realized I forgot to fold my hands. I quickly corrected myself hoping God didn't see me and that I wouldn't have to start all over; during rehearsals they made me start all over from the main entrance if I forgot to fold my hands. I guess it was okay because we got to the prayer bench without being turned around. A multitude of flashes, shutter clicks, and clacks accompanied several parents asking us to smile and look straight ahead. The congregation began to read, or more so chanted in Latin. I didn't understand anything, so I just waited for Sister Mary Hannah to glare at us; that was our cue to say, "God Hear Us." We only deferred from our script when Father Gleason ended the congregational chant with a firm "Amen," to which we all said "Amen" in unison. I liked that part, I felt like the sudden increase in volume ensured that God heard us. At this point, we left our knees to the altar and Father Gleason, who stood perched at the top of an ivory stone pulpit. I wondered if anyone ever fell when climbing those elaborate stairs. He descended to a table with a variety of chalices. When we reached him, we received a quarter-sized wafer imprinted with a cross. I scooped mine almost directly from his hand to my mouth, as I thought, "Hope I'm not hurting you too bad Jesus." Still not quite sure why I was asked to eat the body of Christ. When I returned to the front aisle to watch the Father drink the blood of Christ, glad he handled that part of the ceremony, I caught a glimpse of my mother's stare. She surveyed me with both adoration and satisfaction. For her, this was one of my last "firsts"; she had caught me after my first steps, smiled with me for my first smile, saw me spit out my first food, and heard me utter my first incoherent words. Now, it was the first time I declared a belief in God.

Father Gleason's voice boomed, "Join me as we share in the Holy Eucharist."* I directed my attention toward him as he started to signal our exit. Sister Mary Hannah walked along the side aisle, leading the girls out. As an altar boy arrived at our aisle to escort us out, I was hit with two waves of emotion. The first came with the words "I've done it!"

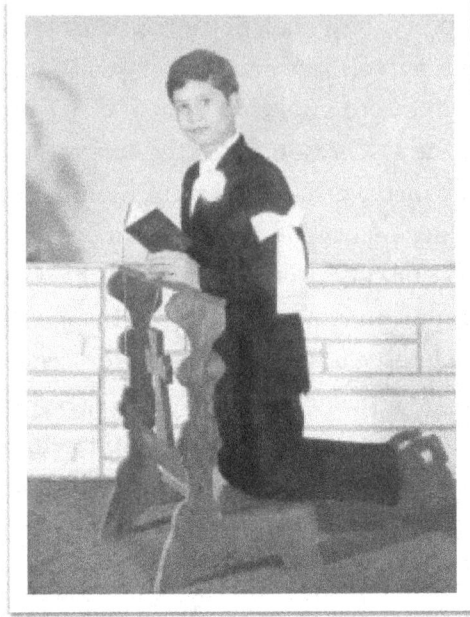

Over-joyed at the prospect of becoming the child of a real-life superhero, an all-knowing power who was willing to love me and capable of keeping me safe going forward. With this, I was met with a second wave of emotion, my head started to swim. Struck by dizziness; like the snowy appearance of an old TV set in pre-cable and satellite days, every figure in front of me started to phase out. My ears filled with a deafening crescendo that drowned out the voices of the crowd. When it subsided all, I could hear was a muffled garble, I only identified as the priest's voice, because he ended it, yet another long drawn out "Amen." People's bodies became an outline of silhouetted figures as the snowy white background changed to a hue of red, and gray then faded to black. "Are you okay?" my mother asked, holding me in her arms, trying to get me to look into her eyes. I said yes but I knew I wasn't. I began dreading going to Sunday Mass; every week the spells struck, worsening every time the priest would ring that hellish bell commencing Communion. Trying not to pass out, pinballing off the final two rows of pews, I made my way up to the altar. Then I returned to my seat, placed my head on the pew's banister in front of me, and began praying fervently till it passed. It was an unrelenting pain. Was God trying to tell me something? Was He rejecting me? Was I "**Rosemary's Baby**"? [28]

One Sunday morning, I refused to attend Mass altogether. Naturally concerned for my well-being, my mom asked me why I didn't want to go. "I'm not feeling well Ma," I replied, pulling the covers a little higher over my head, "Just wanna stay in bed." I became afraid of attending what I believed, at the time, to be God's house. I was raised and indoctrinated to believe that which I now know to be a compromised lie.

* The Catholic rite of Holy Communion parallels pre-Christian Greco-Roman and Egyptian rituals that involved eating the body and blood of a god.

Catholic holidays and myths, such as Christmas, Easter, and Mardi Gras, graph onto the timeline of pre-Christian fertility festivals.

The **Catholic practice of praying to saints** has been **called "de-facto idolatry"** and is even **a relic of goddess worship.**

I-H-S on the Gold Chalice encasing the so-called holy Eucharists (symbolizing the sun-god) stood for 3 pagan demi-gods:

I for **Isis, H** for **Horus,** and **S** for **Seb. Babylonian Trinity Sun gods** transforming the unholy ceremony into a **"Black Mass."**

According to the Bible**,** it's an **Abomination,** to mix ancient Egyptian and Roman paganism with Christianity.

(It's like mixing the pure water of the Gospel with the rancid oil of this secular world.)

*A few traditions in the Roman Catholic Church can be traced back to pagan cults, rites, and deities.

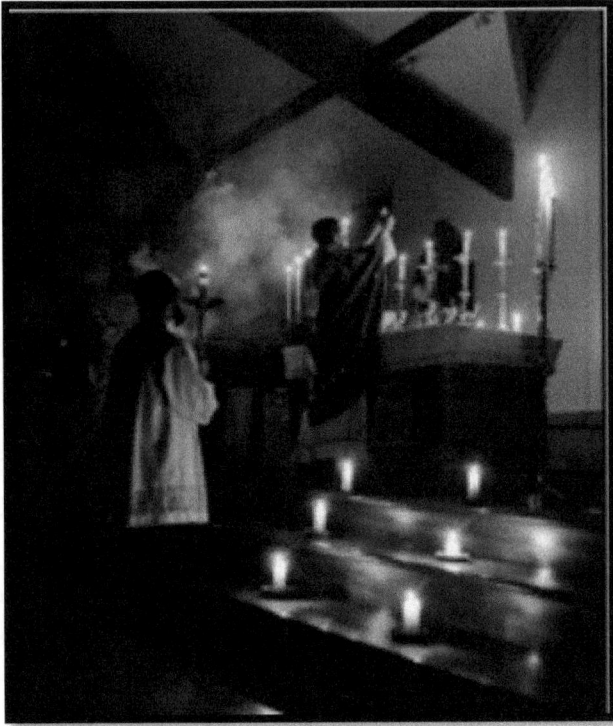

https://bigthink.com/the-present/pagan-roots-of-catholicism
"I am committed to exposing and confronting the evils that persist, guided by a spirit of love and compassion. My sincere hope is to help others break free from the dark, ritualistic chains of religious oppression that once bound me, so that they too can experience the same deliverance." The Lord Almighty is too great to be confined to a box.

Thank you and May the LORD bless you with His divine revelation. My dear **Catholic brothers and sisters,** please do not be offended; but prayerfully take the time to read the following:

Apologetic Disclosure...

TRANSITION

*In this Chapter Four of our book, entitled "Black Mass", we delved into the historical interplay between paganistic Roman ideologies and their potential influence on the Catholic Church.

The intent behind this exploration is to shed light on the complexities of historical development and their counterproductive potential for cultural cross-pollination, while acknowledging the sensitive nature of this subject matter. It is important to note that our aim in not to undermine or question the foundations of the Catholic faith, but rather foster understanding and encourage dialogue surrounding the evolution of religious institutions. We understand that the topic of pagan influences on the Catholic Church can evoke strong emotions and concerns, particularly among those who hold deep religious convictions. The concept of a "Black mass" is highly controversial, as it refers to a ritual that mocks and distorts the traditional Catholic Mass. We recognize the profound reverence that Catholics hold for the Eucharist and the Mass, and we hope to assure readers that our intention is not to promote or endorse any disrespectful interpretations. Our purpose is to encourage thoughtful reflection on the historical dynamics that have shaped religious institutions, while also acknowledging the ongoing commitment of the Catholic Church to its core beliefs. To be fair, we must acknowledge that Protestant churches, as well as other denominations and sects of Christianity have also been tainted by paganistic infiltration. In light of potential concerns raised by our readers, we strongly emphasize that the exposure of Pagan influences on the Catholic Church is a scholarly endeavor aimed at enhancing our understanding of history and its impact on contemporary religious practices. Historical events can vary, and our goal is to present a balanced and well-researched perspective that stimulates thoughtful dialogue rather than division.

*In conclusion, we offer this **apologetic disclosure** as a sincere expression of our respect for diverse perspectives, and our commitment to fostering meaningful conversations about the intricate interplay between history, culture, and faith. We empathize with the potential sensitivities surrounding the topic of "Black Mass" and its implications, with the sincere hope that our readers will approach this chapter with an open mind and full understanding of our intentions.*

Invitation:

Please feel free to email me directly with any questions,
and to engage in further discussions or provide constructive feedback,
as your insights are valuable in shaping a more comprehensive
understanding of this intricate topic.
Thank you.

Sincerely,
Chaplain Nelson Colón
ChaplainNC@Gmail.com
New Creation Concepts

Chapter Five

Like Father Like Son

July 1970

I wore my Easter best for a four-hour flight to Puerto Rico. The same polyester suit from a year ago grew tighter around my shoulders and wrists but still fit if I let the pants ride a few inches below my waist so they could reach my shoes and hide my socks until I sat. This made me obsessively self-conscious when I needed to sit; not knowing that high waters were an acceptable fashion in P.R. Awkward silence accompanied me and the people adjacent to me who I named arm-rest allies; every half an hour we'd glance at each other yielding the armrest to each other rather than sharing or fighting over it. I was only 12, I imagined the negotiations would have likely been more difficult if I were an adult. I used what I believed to be my childish good looks to get my way and stared back with wonderment. Their eyes studied me on occasion; wondering if I knew that I would soon wilt in a suit I so proudly wore. I would toss them a smile hoping they'd say something, but they would just resume staring at the worn headrest in front of them.

Unbeknownst to me, the smoldering sun eagerly awaited me at the terminal. I was just praying to arrive there okay. I distinctly remember hearing some news reporter announcing on tv of a hijacking which occurred just two years ago.

In 1968, a group of pro-independence activists hijacked a Pan American airplane en route from New York to Puerto Rico. The hijackers demanded the release of Puerto Rican political prisoners and an end to U.S. colonialism in Puerto Rico. The incident lasted several days and ultimately ended with the release of the hostages and the hijackers' surrender.

My cheeks hurt from the involuntary smile that painted my face every time I looked down at my clean suit, hoping that good old Dad would be impressed, and see me for the man I was becoming. I believed my "Papi" sent for me because of the dozen letters I wrote him pleading for an opportunity, but, as I later found out, it was my mother. She knew how much I missed him and how much I craved his attention even though I would never say it. I could hear the countless phone conversations that carried through the walls of my room late past my bedtime, reminiscent of the yells exchanged in PR years ago. "No me lo deje solo. Cuidalo ... Tu Hijo te necesita."[29] The pilot announced, "On your left, you will see San Juan, we will arrive on time at 3:15 p.m." I begged the gray-haired woman beside me for a glance out her window. When she conceded, I carefully leaned over her to see the city but all I could see were mounds of green with occasional strips of gray and brown which I assumed were roads; cars moved along them much like ants across the corners of my kitchen counter. Where were the buildings?

TRANSITION

The concrete jungle I had become so accustomed to being a world away. Upon my arrival at *San Juan* Airport, I could smell the heat, suffocated by my shirt collar. My eyebrows tried valiantly to keep the sweat out of my eyes but to no avail. The sting tried to steal my smile, but I was determined to wear it as I walked into an open space by the main gate, hoping my father might be in crowds of waving people. I scanned the masses for my father's face, trying to add three years to it so I could accurately identify him. I even waved at a few strangers who were confused at my fake recognition and forced smile. It was becoming increasingly difficult to keep, beads of sweat soaking into my shoulders; I felt as if I were a fully saturated sponge; I wished my mother was there to wring me out. To alleviate the surmounting pressure. I took the deepest breath I could muster but only felt further inflated as if I would burst.

At the crucial moment, I heard a woman's voice repeating "Nelson, Nelson!" and turned my gaze to her. I had never seen her before, but her eyes locked on me with familiarity. She was a short, stocky, well-built UFC-type woman with a white short-sleeve nylon blouse, shorts, and sandals. She was attractive but had to be tough to hang with my father. She looked like she could handle herself if it ever came to that. She looked at me with some worry, wondering if I had melted underneath my clothes; immediately peeling my jacket off, "Dame tu Jacket." She added an "Aye Dios Mio!" and it reminded me a little of my mother. I liked that my mother called out to God when she was in distress, but when this woman said it, it was more like a curse word. She added, "Estas lleno de sudor. Ven bebe agua."[30] as she led me to the nearest water fountain. I still didn't know who she was, or more importantly who she was to my father. "Hola I'm Dominga, your father's wife", seeming like she just had read my mind, and then immediately breaking out in broken English, "You look like your picture." I wish I had known this before, but it appeared that my father had remarried and started anew in the same suburb of Ponce. Where I used to ride my trikes. I wondered if he still had them rusting out somewhere, but I didn't dare ask. My dad's new wife seemed nice enough to guarantee my trust. At least until we approached a small, single-propeller job that only seated six. I really thought we were going to get in a car, so I silently pleaded with the most convincing facial expression of worry I could muster.

To no avail, we boarded yet another plane which I knew required that I perform the same take-off ritual I did in New York. As we prepared to lift off from San Juan, after only arriving there moments ago, I kissed my right hand with my eyes closed and recited the prayer I thought Sister Mary Hannah had crafted, "Our Father who art in Heaven ..."

I finished the prayer as all Catholics had to, by gesturing a cross with my right hand, hoping I did it in the right order. I must have got it wrong because as soon as we lifted off the runway the seats shook as if we would drop right back down to the ground. A part of me hoped it would happen sooner rather than later, when we were higher up and death was more certain. I watched out the windows as the cars, roads, and buildings became less frequent, replaced by mounds of green. "Do people live down there?" I asked Dominga. "Yes, that's Ponce.", she replied. I fixed my eyes on the floor for the remaining minutes of the flight, watching the screws in the steel floorboard rattle beside my feet. Once in Ponce, Dominga drove me to the urbanization, called Glenview Gardens. As she swooped into the driveway, I saw that it was a nice bright peach home. It didn't have a white picket fence, but it was clean and comfortable. More than I could say for the old, broken-down, roach-infested apartment buildings I could never get used to in Bushwick.

TRANSITION

As I waited for my father to arrive home from his job, Dominga tried to make me feel at home by insisting I fill up on soda crackers and extra salty butter. As a result, I requested at least four glasses of water, probably necessary anyway. I was likely bordering on dehydration and heat stroke after sweating through my suit. Despite this, I didn't change my clothes. I was trying desperately to hold out until my father got home so he could see me in my new duds. I hoped for a swollen smile and a bone-crushing hug.

After a few hours, I finally heard my dad's van pull up the driveway. My stomach tightened with nervous apprehension, as I watched him climb down from his van through the kitchen window. He wore a blue construction helmet and mustard overalls. Bypassing the kitchen, my father walked directly into his bedroom, "Dominga, Dónde está mi camisa roja?" Don't know why he was asking her for his red shirt, guess it was clean in contrast to his dusty overall. He conversed with Dominga for a few minutes in their bedroom. I could overhear the common conversation that lived within the walls every day. "But I was new to this home? Has he forgotten me?" I thought. "Does he know I'm here?" I had almost convinced myself to get up and approach their bedroom, when my father walked out, taking a step back as if startled by me. He inquired "Nelson?" as he walked about me. I didn't know whether to run up to him or just wait for him to come to me. Before I could choose, he pulled me to him with a grip that seemed unbreakable and kissed me, the bristles of his beard digging into my cheek and neck. He said, "Que grande estas mi Hijo!" He firmly grasped my arms and looked deeply into the green eyes my mama had given me. I smiled but didn't laugh and wasn't sure if I should or could. "Dios te bendiga! Then attempted to show me he could speak English as well, "Wow...It's really good to see you mijo." Sounding a bit choked up, turning to Dominga who had now turned her attention to the dirty dishes in the kitchen sink, "Mira, what do you think of my son, isn't he a good-looking boy?" Dominga chimed "Yes, but he doesn't look much like you. He must have come out looking more like his mother", with a smirk. My father must not have found that very amusing because he didn't even respond. As he began working his way to the bathroom to shower, Dominga quickly added, "He's a very fine boy", her smirk receding. That evening, I did not rest easy, even after I got my mother on the phone and assured her, I was well. Dominga and my father moved about the house at all hours of the night exchanging unpleasantries that I could barely make out through the walls. I wondered if it was normal or if my presence caused the strife.

The next morning, Dominga offered to take me to a pool in the neighborhood. We were there from open to sundown. It wasn't until I was in the shower that I realized I got too much sun, every drop of water triggered a stinging, burning sensation deep in my skin. Three swift knocks came at the door of the bathroom, so I hurried to get the last of Johnson's shampoo out of my hair and eyes. My mother had packed it for me because I never wanted to use any other, the smell wasn't the same. I regularly pointed out that they say it's tear-free, but it still stung; intentionally getting in my eye so I could show my mother how irritated my eyes could get, "See mom, it's not tear-free." Three heavier knocks came at the door as I whipped the towel through my hair and wrapped the towel around my waist. I didn't have time to dry off the rest of me, so I opened the door while still dripping wet, puddles forming at my feet. My father stood there, in his full work gear, his face and forearms covered in thick soot, work boots accompanied by a subtle trail of mud he inadvertently dragged in. He had just got back from work and expected the bathroom to be available. "Que Carajo! What the hell were you doing in there, muchacho, that took you so long?" I didn't know how to answer. "Well, you deaf, answer me?" "Showering Papi," I replied. As he huffed a deep and violent breath and took me by the back of my neck and gave me to Dominga. She attempted to soothe me, escorting me to the fridge for a bottle of green gel. I didn't know what it was, there was no label, but when she applied it to my back she said, "It's aloe honey, aloe." Her kindness snapped me out of the shock from the confrontation I had just had with my father; I started to bawl. She offered her shoulder, and I took it, "I know, I know." she said in her attempt to comfort me.

My father was a confusing contradiction, and therefore a mystery to me. He would fluctuate from kind and caring, to cursing and cruel in a moment with no obvious reason. After that encounter, I became fearful of him for the first time, avoiding him altogether when he got home from work, and making sure I was nowhere near his bathroom. A part of me wanted to forget it ever happened but felt like I had to remember so I could avoid his unmerited wrath. After a week passed, and the newness of my presence wore off and I was left to fend for myself and manage my own time. I liked it! Dominga resumed her usual daily routine, leaving in the mornings to see her sister down the block, and then heading to the Plaza in "el Pueblo" [31] to buy groceries and pick up some cuchifritos. I watched kids my age making their way down to the common grounds with baseball bats. I chose to remain in the house in front of the only fan. I would watch whatever cartoons were on at the time; one of my favorites was The Flintstones, in Spanish they were translated into "Los Pica Piedras." My father would eventually get home covered in dust wearing his blue construction cap, taking his muddy boots off by the door, and tossing them onto the marquesina (patio) tiled floor. Hating to find me home just watching tv all day he abruptly asked me, "What are you doing in the house?" Digging into his wallet and coming out with a $10 bill, he continued with his motivational coaching, "Toma... Be a man, go outside and take a walk to the store or something, don't just stay in the house." My father's legacy was just bent on teaching me Puro Machismo 101. A Puerto Rican Rite-of-Passage. One day we went to visit my half-sister, Gloria, who was baptizing her daughter that evening. That was the night I had my first drink. I was always very shy around people, especially when I didn't know them very well. My father must have noticed my uneasiness because he took me over to a table that was stocked with liquor bottles of every kind, and a variety of sodas. He commenced to mix himself a drink and told me to watch very carefully. He poured from a bottle labeled 'Bacardi -Rum,' over two ice cubes into a third of the glass. Then he filled the remaining two-thirds up with 'Coca-Cola'. He quickly stirred it with his index finger, licked it, claimed it was perfect, then handed the drink over to me. My father then proceeded to instruct me on how to drink the concoction he called a "Cuba Libre." Told me to sip it slowly, that I would get used to it. Gave me permission to help myself to another, after I've acquired a taste for it. I remember the drink tasted a bit strong at first, but my Pops was right, after I got beyond the strange taste I began to enjoy it.

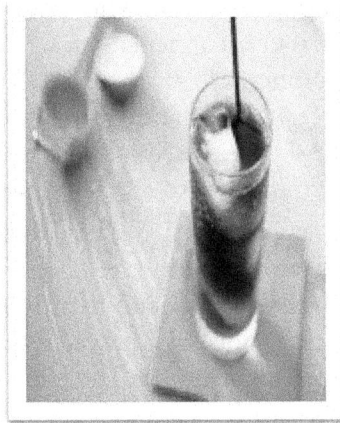

After I had downed the first drink, I felt kind of funny. I wasn't sure if I should have had another, but to impress my father, and prove to him that I was paying attention to his explicit instructions, I did! The second one was better than the first. The strong taste was gone, and the funny sensation in my head began to feel good.

I was no longer afraid of my strange surroundings. Everyone was drinking similar concoctions, and everyone seemed to be experiencing the same carefree, happy- go-lucky feelings that I was. By my third drink, I was so euphoric, that I even found myself dancing a Bolero[32] with a tall, slim cinnamon-colored girl who was almost twice my size. I must have been making a fool of myself, because my father suddenly intervened, and blurted out in a half-drunken slur "I think it's time we were leaving mijo, Vamos muchacho." I yelled out a "Buenas Noche" to everyone as I was being dragged out by my Pops, and managed to even wink, and blow a kiss to my pretty young dancing partner. I recall, as if it were in a dream, her returning an approving smile. My father just seemed to mumble something under his breath, as he helped me into his van, waved to everybody, climbed onto the driver's seat, and drove off.

I don't remember getting home, for I blacked out in the van, and my father must have carried me to bed. I began to get my fill of what I later learned to be bed spins. It was like floating endlessly on an ocean, and from the fear of drowning, I had to constantly raise my head up for air. Well, I must have gotten seasick because, after about five minutes of that self-induced torture, I ran to the toilet and spilled my guts out. I think it was Dominga who, once again like an angel of mercy, came to my rescue helping me off my knees, cleaning me up, and getting me back into bed. I realize now she was rather adept at providing this kind of care, attuned to the signs that would cue her in on when to intervene and when to carefully observe me. Didn't realize till later that my father had given her plenty of practice.

The next day, I discovered the true meaning of a hangover. "God, why do people put themselves through such torture?" I thought, is this what it means to be an adult. For a few moments of bliss, one must pay with nightmarish consequences and then wake up to the aftermath of this. My head felt twice its original size, every sound magnified until every noise became a deafening mind-splitting reverberation. Dominga walked into the room with a glass of orange juice, and two aspirins, and told me that it would help if I took them. My father just found it funny and made a big joke about it. I, on the other hand, felt it was no laughing matter. Had a bad case of the runs and lost all my appetite. My head was completely fogged in, affecting my vision and perspective, leaving a very vital part of it in the clouds somewhere. I hung around all day in this cloud, trying to recuperate somehow, regretting ever touching the stuff, and swearing that I would never touch it again.

My conviction didn't last, for some days later I went out and attended a dance some teens in the neighborhood invited me to. After what I thought was a good time, I got back to my father's house late that night, stinking drunk. I don't remember how I even got home, but the following day I was dealing with a hangover, once again, and felt like an utter fool. My father didn't seem to mind at all. He seemed to actually condone my actions. After all, guess I was beginning to meet more of his expectations by being more like him, a mucho macho-man. My father encouraged it, by giving me enough money each week, to get lost and stay out of his hair.

Summer vacation was finally over, and I flew back home. Arriving at JFK, my mother couldn't even recognize me. In contrast to how I was before, a short, chubby, timid little boy, in two months I had morphed into a tall, skinny, arrogant young man. My Adam's apple also magically popped out. As dramatic as the change in my physical appearance was, there was something even more different about my mental state. Something dark had entered me, reaching down into the deep recesses of my soul. The evil in my life had now grown to near maturity and the wicked seeds planted during my early childhood were now steadily growing into thickets and thistles of sin. I began having a very unhealthy attitude toward myself, as well as toward others. My mother had recently moved and being the new kid on the block gave me the opportunity to make some new friends. My drastic change in height made me more acceptable to the older crowd so I began lying about my age. I was able to pass for fifteen, even though I was only twelve. From the peer pressure of this older crowd with whom I hung out, I picked up the nasty habit of smoking, as well as indulging in further alcohol consumption.

TRANSITION

One day, attempting to impress my new neighborhood friends, I invited a couple of them up to the apartment, after coming home early from school. They were all heavy drinkers, and I couldn't bore them with Kool-Aid, so I hit my mother's private stock of alcoholic beverages. The guys were content in having a couple of shots of rum each, but of course, I wasn't satisfied with that alone, so in my attempt to outdrink them, I mixed one part anisette with a shot of J&B Scotch Whiskey took a deep breath, and whisked it all down, as my newly found drinking-buddies stared in disbelief. If that wasn't enough, I immediately followed that down with a cold can of beer, as a chaser. I remember my buddies telling me, "Hey man, you're going to get sick!" I just shrugged it off, and responded, "Not me, I can handle it!" We all left the apartment, and within the next hour, I literally blacked out. Completely left my mental senses, but not my physical actions.

The following day my buddies ran down to me all the crazy things that had ensued. How I made a spectacle of myself, acting as a wild dog, foaming at the mouth, running after the girls on the block, and knocking hats off the heads of little old men. When I finally started coming down off the drunken high, I was discovered sitting on my stoop in a senseless stupor by my landlord Mr. Rodolico. A very nice Italian man: a widower who loved smoking cigars. He practically carried me up the stairs, fed me some black coffee, and watched out for me till my mom got home. When my family got a load of me that evening, they all swore I had taken some kind of drug, other than alcohol, but my wise mother knew better. She immediately checked out her private stock of liquor bottles, which were all a little underneath the imaginary line she positively knew they were all filled up to.

My mom led me to believe I was getting away with it, and just let me sleep it off, but the next day she let me have it, both barrels. "I knew it!" she exploded, "I should have never let you go visit your father. He's been nothing but trouble in my life, since the very beginning, and now it pains me to see that what I have been dreading is starting to come true. You are beginning to be just like your father, 'Un Sin Verguenza'!"[33] She just stared at me for a very long minute as if I were him, totally creeping me out. Then just went on and on in her native Spanish dialect, and so I didn't dare try to argue with her. After all, I began to recognize the distinct possibility that **she might be right.**

Chapter Six

My teens were a blur. In the words of one of my favorite Motown groups, the Temptations, * my head most of the time just felt like a "Ball of Confusion" for most of this period.

The Temptations-An American vocal group known for their success with Motown Records during the 1960s and 1970s. With their distinct harmonies, choreography, & flashy wardrobe, the group was highly influential in the evolution of R&B and Soul music.

I moved around in a semi-conscious state of alcoholic inebriation coupled with various levels of drug addiction. I was already smoking marijuana, popping pills, and dropping acid like it was going out of style. Amid my drug escapades, I could almost hear the voice of my mother reciting the golden rules in my early years of innocence, almost prophetically encouraging me to "Stay Clean."

At thirteen, to keep from continually being victimized, I joined a gang called the *Homicide Laws*. We were always engaged in some turf war with other gangs in the hood. One night a major rumble broke out between our ally gangs in Bushwick and some rival gangs in Bed-Stuy. They were throwing bricks from the rooftops of the buildings and shooting at us. I felt the heat of one bullet as it whistled by my left ear, as I dove under a parked car. After that close call with death, I began undertaking other forms of recreation. Between the ages of fourteen and fifteen, two major things happened; I lost my virginity to a beautiful, black Amazonian girl by the name of Norma, and started hanging out with my newfound neighborhood sidekick Carlos, who might as well have been a son of the devil, aka "Ace-of-Diamonds."

He took me under his wing and adopted me into his O-Gangsta-Apprenticeship-Program, earning me the nickname "Jack-of-Spades" and introducing me to harder drugs like methadone. Carlos was a couple of years older, but a lot more experienced in street life, teaching me how to "geese"; the art of "breaking and entering" into factories

84

and facilities in the industrial area of South Side Brooklyn. My brother Cano, tired of my sneaking into our small 2-bedroom apartment in the wee hours of the morning, saw fit to chastise me early one evening on my way to hang out. Our poor tired mother had already gone to bed as we got into a scuffle.

Cano was separated from his wife and was temporarily staying with us back in Bushwick again. He chose to lay down the law and proceeded to tell me I was not going out that night. I think I told him where he could go, and he turned me around and stopped me dead in my tracks with a right hook to my lip. As I attempted to reciprocate the favor by grabbing a lamp from my dresser, we were separated by our sleep-woke mother who stood in the middle like a struggling referee. "Boy, you lucky Mami got in the way I was about to knock you out!" my brother shouted at me. I took advantage of the opportunity and ran out of the apartment onto the streets, wiping the fresh blood oozing from my busted lip with the back of my hand. Carlos conveniently lived just one block over on Gates Avenue. He was waiting for me on the corner and helped nurse my lip back to health with a cold bottle of Wild Irish Rose. My brother Cano and I never got into a physical fight before, it was the first and last time. He was instantly convicted, the weight of remorse crashing over him. The guilt must have been overwhelming, because he sat down and wrote me a note, leaving it on my bed. It simply read: "Nelson, I'm so sorry..."

Later that night, as I quietly crept back into the dark, lifeless apartment, I flicked on the light in my room and there it was—the note. Still slightly buzzed from the wine and pot, I could feel the tears welling up as I read his words. They cut through the haze, and I couldn't hold back the flood of emotions that followed.

NELSON COLÓN

My big bro had five years on me. He was only seventeen when he got married, and I think it was mainly to get out of the house and away from our mother's excessive nagging. In my mid-teens he and his older wife Sandy had me come to live with them on the nicer side of Brooklyn on Park Slope, in a nice Brownstone right by Prospect Park. I had made it into HS of Art & Design because of my artistic talent and was doing well in my freshman year until I became derailed by my hang-out buddies.

Soon thereafter I started cutting school and hanging out, drinking' and drugging' again. That's when my brother intervened and took me in and away from the negative element of Bushwick. He also helped me in my transfer to a nearby trade school called Automotive High in Greenpoint, Brooklyn. It was a lot closer to Park Slope, eliminating the long tedious train commute to mid-Manhattan every day. I quickly cleaned up my act and even joined the Automotive Track Team. Brought home a trophy after participating in the Cross-Country Brooklyn Championships and felt like I was on "Top of the world Ma!" I was on the bright side of the Moon, for a change, and got a real sweet taste of a normal healthy functional lifestyle. Unfortunately, it didn't last. A year later, my brother broke up with his wife, and I ended up back on the other side of the tracks again. I took it hard, fell into a deep state of depression, and it was just a matter of time before my old crew began seeking me out and influencing me again. I was sixteen, and inevitably I did what I had sworn I would never do.

The final initiation into the tightly knit crew occurred when Carlos gave me my first shot of heroin. With the dexterity of a doctor, he initiated my first skin-pop. It wasn't long thereafter that I was turned on to mainlining "speedballs" which was a dangerous mixture of heroin and cocaine. The sensation was like a roller-coaster ride, with the cocaine lurching my heart upward with an explosive adrenaline rush, in conjunction with the heroin immediately kicking in, and abruptly crashing me down into a deep nod. I was hooked! Living for the weekend became an ongoing habitual ritual of my newfound religion. Discoing Friday nights to certain clubs throughout lower Manhattan like The Loft and The Gay-rage. After 'breaking night' and having breakfast in the city we usually would shoot up to Brentwood, Long Island. Where we would hang out at 'Uncle Felty's pad, a middle-aged gay predator who would tantalize us young teens with money, drugs, and free entry to well-known dance clubs to help fulfill his lascivious agenda. We would continue abusing our minds and bodies with more drugs that were made readily available by everyone that would attend these extended weekend-long parties. The menu contained appetizers like amphetamines, mescaline, and marijuana. The main entrée consisted of cocaine with wine, liquor, and Kool-Aid acid punch refreshment chasers. I wouldn't make it back to Brooklyn until late Sunday night. I would crawl into bed, and go into my comatose mode, in a desperate attempt to recoup, regroup and reset. Come Friday night, I will do it all over again. What insanity! That's pretty much how I spent my last summer vacay, just prior to entering my Senior High School year.

On my first day back at Automotive High, I felt like I never came down from my high but was still tripping on acid. My brain cells were fried from all those wild weekend ventures, and now waiting in the school cafeteria listening for that school bell's hellish ring was outright mental torture. After what seemed like an eternity, I began cursing aloud at the bell for not having rung. "F'ing Ring Already!" The bell seemed totally indifferent as if it were rebelliously retaliating, remaining in stubborn silence. Startled students were all staring at me seemingly annoyed for having abruptly awoken them from their semi-conscious state of mind. Desperate, I attempted to flee the torture chamber from hell and challenged one of the teachers guarding one of the exits by the eastern wall. Weighing only 125 pounds, I stood in defiance as I challenged that 250-pound, 6-foot-plus Phys-Ed teacher, demanding him to, "Get out of the way!" At first, he completely ignored me, until I commenced to take my jacket off and threw it down on the ground before him. He must have quickly realized 'this kid must be on something' because he just simply stepped aside and looked the other way.

TRANSITION

Running out of the school and into the street, I ran by a former classmate walking up the stone stairs who shouted after me, "Hey Nelson, where are you going man? The school's this way!" I didn't respond, I just kept running. I used to run the track for Automotive High, and most of the workouts Mr. Cole, our coach, used to put us through were extensive and very strenuous, but this run was different. It wasn't tiresome like most runs. The farther I ran the more refreshed and invigorated I felt. It was like I was trying to set myself free from everything that might have had a hold on me. Everything in this world seemed to be so controlling, so manipulatively evil; school, family, friends, and everyone seemed to be all striving for the same monetary gain, position, power, and status. It was all so futile. I wanted to get as far away from everyone, and everything caught up in this systematic Rat Race we've all accepted as life.

I felt so dirty and degraded by this world, so lost, so empty, that I was desperate for some real fulfillment, yearning to be clean, complete, with some true direction. Desperately needed something to give my senseless life some meaning, and I wasn't sure what it was. Frantic, I began running ceaselessly, seeking liberation from the clutches of this malevolent world. Stripping myself of everything which was inhibiting, I made a feeble attempt to purge myself from all lasciviousness and degradation. In my most fervent yearning, I craved GOD ... to see me pure, unblemished, and unashamed. Akin to Aam and Eve in the Garden before their fall from grace. Even amidst this vivid acid flashback, it felt as though GOD Himself was reaching down into the deep recesses of my soul-stirring me awake and revealing the profound depth of my desperate need of the Savior.

An authoritative voice entered my head interjecting and correcting, "Only I can truly make you Clean." I ran with a single-minded urgency, driven by an overpowering need to escape. My frantic pace didn't slow until I found myself at the dock of the bay in Williamsburg, Brooklyn. The cool night air and the rhythmic sound of the water were a stark contrast to the turmoil I'd left behind. On a whim, I wandered into a nearby playground, where the simplicity of hopscotch became my unexpected refuge. I leaped and skipped, the childish game a brief, joyful distraction from my heavier thoughts. Afterward, I sat beneath the gushing water of an open hydrant, letting the refreshing spray wash over me, the droplets mingling with the sweat and tears. It was in that moment, drenched and exhilarated, that an overwhelming sense of elation surged through me. The day was alive with possibilities, and for the first time in what felt like ages, I became blissfully awakened and aware of the present.

Then the demons materialized, dressed in blue uniforms, they came impersonating policemen, but I saw through their facade. I attempted to get away, but when I turned the corner to run another squad car cut me off dead in my tracks. They came out of their patrol cars and overtook me. One of the officers took his nightstick out and was ready to hit me with it when I looked sternly into his eyes. God must have convicted him because the officer immediately looked ashamed and put his nightstick away. The other officer wasn't as sympathetic, grabbing and slamming me against their patrol car. He took hold of my hands and handcuffed them behind my back. "Now, where do you think you're going without your clothes, huh buddy?" the officer asked mockingly as he pulled a blanket out of the trunk, wrapped it around me, and placed me into the back of his cruiser.

The next thing I knew they had me strapped down onto a bed at some nearby hospital. I was face down with both feet tied together with restraints and strapped to one end of the bed, with my hands still handcuffed behind me. They left me there hog-tied, for what seemed like an eternity until the transport finally arrived. When they untied me and tried to get me to walk, I collapsed. My legs had gone completely numb from lack of circulation. They called for the orderly who sat me in a wheelchair and loaded me onto the medical transport, which took me straight to Kings County Hospital.

Arriving at King's County, they placed me in a white frayed hospital gown. A Shrink in a white lab coat gave me a psychiatric evaluation and administered an injection. A couple of orderlies resembling football linemen strapped me onto a wooden wheelchair and escorted me upstairs to the mental ward. Upon entering the ward, it was like watching an eerie scene from *Night of the Living Dead*. There were people walking aimlessly about, stopping for a moment to stare at me as they swayed side to side, and then continued their programmed route like computerized robots. Some attempted to greet me, but what would come out of their drooling mouths was but a slur. There was one that looked very familiar to me, a young man about my age, probably someone from my neighborhood, but I just couldn't place him. I was in what they called the Dayroom. Some guys were watching TV, while others played cards or dominoes. Some were just strewn about the floor, either asleep, staring catatonically at the walls, or at nothing.

There was a long hallway where the shower stalls and restrooms were. Adjoining the end of the hall was a huge dorm with cots lined up and down the room. I was told by another big male orderly, acting more like a bouncer, that the Dorm was off-limits during the day and sarcastically added, "That's why we call this the DAYROOM!" as he escorted me back to it. I was beginning to feel the effect of the injection. Exhausted, but not wanting to lie down on that filthy floor, I put two white plastic chairs together and laid across them in a fetal position. I escaped into la-la land for a while, in and out of sleep, but at one point was disturbed by a high shrill scream that seemed very familiar to me. As much as I wanted to look up to see who had screamed, immediately followed by hysterical weeping, I just could not seem to shake off the deep sleep which had taken me captive. I felt like Rip Van Winkle in a land far, far away.

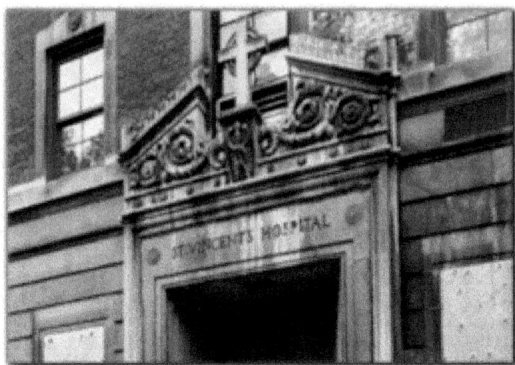

Little did I know that the scream and weeping I had heard belonged to my dear mother. She, along with the rest of my family, had finally been notified by the authorities. My brother Cano, thankfully, was there to calm her down. Although, when Cano peered through the looking glass and saw the state I was in, he joined Mami's cries. To be strong, Cano quickly composed himself, as he consoled our dear mother.

Thereafter witnessing the jail-like conditions at Kings County, he fought like a mad-man on a mission and got me transferred to a private hospital. In two weeks, after cutting through some red tape, he was able to relocate me to St. Vincent's Hospital in lower Manhattan. In contrast to the city facilities that were made available to me at Kings County, this mental ward was like heaven. St. Vincent's was a whole lot more humane, clean, and with a touch of class. We had our own private rooms which we shared with only one other roommate, instead of sleeping in one big dorm which reeked of pungent body and foot odor. Despite the improved conditions, I didn't respond well to treatment. The Psychiatrists diagnosed me with "Paranoid Schizophrenia" and doped me up with Thorazine. After four months they offered up one last option for me to start Electro-Shock Therapy or E.C.T. (Electroconvulsive Therapy), to which in desperation, my family consented, and they proceeded. After what seemed to be endless sessions of ECT, I didn't really show any positive changes. They ran electric currents through my brain hoping to dislodge some negative mindset, but all it accomplished was causing me to have seizures and serious migraines. My brain was literally fried. It was totally barbaric and straight out of the medieval ages. I felt like Randle Patrick McMurphy in *One Flew Over the Cuckoo's Nest*.[34] The next available step was to consider having me committed to an Upstate Mental Institution which my family was very opposed to, but seeing no other options open they inevitably began to lose hope. Apparently, it was the perfect scenario and timing for **divine intervention.**

One day during visiting hours, no one from my family had come, but an angel appeared disguised as a cute little old black lady who came just for me. She was staring at me throughout the whole time as other patients were being visited by their families. I was sitting and fidgeting on the sofa trying to watch tv as well as keeping an eye out for any of my family members that may have been arriving late. An hour later, the nurse's station announced via the intercom that visiting hours were over. Patients were walking their guests to the exit doors in the main lobby to say their goodbyes. I was left in the living room area feeling so disappointed no one had come to visit me. I got up from the sofa to return to my room when the earth angel chose to confront me.

Apparently, I was her assignment. She walked over to me, introducing herself as a minister, waving some small object in her hand. It was a small book with a dark green cover. She claimed the LORD had sent her to deliver this to someone, and after observing me sitting alone for the last hour, she knew it was for me. She then handed me a small pocket version of a Gideon's Bible and suggested that I read Psalm 23. She already had placed a small book marker inside the pocket bible making it conveniently easy for me to find. "Please Read this." She said, "It contains God's love letter to you. Read it prayerfully, meditate and reflect on it, and the LORD will speak to you through His Word." My angelic lady then continued to reassure me, "My son, The LORD told me to tell you not to worry for He's **The Good Doctor.** Place your trust in Him, and He will make you well again. **Only He can restore your mind, as well as your soul, and restore you back to your family.**" She then bowed her head and said a quick prayer over me. Afterwards, as my eyes followed her as she slowly walked away, a spark of hope seemed to ignite in me. I believed her. After all, **what other choice did I have?**

TRANSITION

Chapter Seven

Madness to Miraculous

I started to read again. There was a story of a man who was world-renowned, a man respected by his peers, and feared by his advisors. Born to a family of wealth on his way to Jerusalem; he was blinded by a light, thrown to the ground, muddied ... embarrassed and confused, as he called out to the same name I did when stifled by the demon... *"Jesus!"* I know all about those miracles where Jesus spoke a word, and everything was fixed in an instant. Some parts of the miracle in my life were like that, whilst other parts of it took some time, hence my miracle had a beginning that predated its completion by quite some time. My miraculous journey was a bit like the one traveled by the apostle Paul, who spent 17 years being prepared for ministry after he met Jesus on the *Damascus* Road.

I started reading Psalm 23 just as the angelic old lady had instructed, though it wasn't easy—heavy medication blurred my vision, making the words swim before my eyes. But as I persisted, struggling to make sense of the sacred text, something miraculous began to happen. The more I faithfully attempted to read that passage, and as I delved into other captivating stories of Jesus and His 12 Apostles, my vision began to clear, almost as if touched by a divine hand. I also began noticing a positive change in my attitude and started experiencing a strengthening in my soul and spirit. Not only did my vision seem to clear miraculously, but my mind also began exiting from the brain fog.

A faith I had never experienced before was beginning to develop in my inner man. I was responding positively to therapy, getting smaller dosages of medication as a result, and knew it was just a matter of time until I would be released. I had progressed to the point where the doctors felt that I could be granted a pass to be with my family for Thanksgiving weekend.

The Ring: a 2002 American supernatural horror film Directed by Gore Verbinski Screenplay by Ehren Kruger

It was great! My family got together and gave me all the love and support they could muster. I spent Thanksgiving and the entire extended weekend with my family and didn't get back to St. Vincent's till late Sunday evening. Everyone from the ward was on the terrace floor, where they greeted me and asked me how my holiday weekend back home went. I exclaimed, "TERRIFIC!" and went to treat myself to a soda from the ice room. I turned around to exit the room after having gotten a can of soda and a plastic cup filled with ice. Startled by a skimpy, skinny girl with long scraggly black hair, not weighing more than ninety pounds. She was horrible looking, like she just stepped out of the big movie screen of *the Ring.* *

TRANSITION

I threw out a polite "Excuse me," trying to slide past her, but this chick was adamant, like she had planted roots there. I gave it another shot, this time with a bit more edge, "Excuse me... I'd like to pass!" But nope, she just stood her ground, shooting daggers through her eyes. Then, out of nowhere, she started this high-pitched, nails-on-a-chalkboard kind of rant, proclaiming, "WE are all the devil's children, and we're going straight to hell!" The whole demoniac performance, complete with a grin showcasing her greenish-yellow teeth, was like something straight out of a nightmare.

A shiver ran down my spine, every single hair on my body standing at attention. I fought desperately to keep fear from sinking its claws into my heart, but it was a losing battle. I practically bellowed at the girl, "You better get out of my way right now, before I make you eat this can of soda!" Her glare escalated into a fierce, penetrating stare, and her voice transformed into this desperate, Exorcist-worthy, demonically low, bone-chilling tone, "We are the devil's children, and we're all going straight to hell!" Suddenly, she latched onto my left arm, and it was like I'd been hit with a jolt of unearthly energy. It surged through me, a raging electrical fire that made my feet feel like they were melting into the soles of my shoes. On pure instinct, I yanked my arm away from her grasp, the encounter leaving me shaken to the core.

As her desperate fingers clawed at me once more, my instinctive defenses kicked in, propelling my right fist—still gripping that soda can—square into her chest. The can detonated on contact, a burst of chaos echoing the force of my strike. The impact seemed to snatch the wind from her, leaving her doubled over and resembling a macabre marionette, suspended from invisible strings, her haunted gaze fixed downward. Stunned by the impact of my own blow and genuinely worried that I might have inflicted serious harm, I found myself in a frantic state. "Are you alright? I'm sorry, so sorry I hit you, but I warned you... tried to warn you," I blurted out, my concern genuine. Yet, to my astonishment, she swiftly regained her composure and lunged for me once more, that grotesque grin plastered on her face. At this juncture, I abandoned any futile attempts at apology. With the crushed soda can still clenched in my hand, I hurled it to the floor, letting out a primal scream. "No, you can go straight to hell!" I boomed; my patience utterly worn thin. Unleashing a barrage of fists into her flat chest, a relentless assault that finally forced the demoniac to retreat entirely from the doorway.

Bolting past her, I sprinted towards the elevators, my voice echoing through the corridor, "Hey, this place is overrun by demons, run for your lives!" Amid the startling frenzy, a concerned intern hurried over, noticing the distress etched across my face. He asked, "What's wrong?!" I urgently cautioned him not to try and stop me, my finger incessantly pressing the elevator button. "I'm out of here," I forcefully asserted to the young intern, my voice edged with haste, "before that demon girl catches up with me." The gravity in my tone matched the severity of the situation, my palpable fear driving every word.

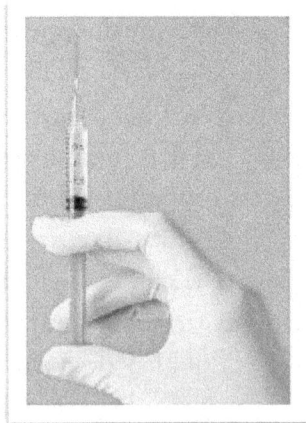

TRANSITION

The elevator doors finally opened, and I jumped in, with the intern closely behind, as he quickly pressed the sixth-floor button for the Mental Ward. He attempted to calm me down, saying, "Everything's going to be all right, Nelson, just put the shoe down." Frazzled in flight and still in fight mode, I didn't realize I had removed one of my earth shoes, holding it up as a weapon. When the elevator doors opened, two other technicians were waiting for us. One had a large hypodermic in his hand ready to shoot me full of some tranquilizing agent, and the other had an opened strait-jacket ready for the custom fitting. Detained and restrained securely within the straitjacket, they carried me to the 'Quiet Room' where they proceeded to inject the sedative right into my rump.

Quickly slipped into a restless, never-ending nightmare; running from evil tormenting spirits in a very dark place from whence there is no escape. Forced back into a pit of despair, self-pity, and depression. Every time the doctors or counselors attempted to ask me what happened that night, I refused to talk about it and quickly diverted to another subject. I concluded that evil is indeed a real force. Despite the unsettling nature of this realization, it strangely provided me with a sense of hope. I realized that if evil truly existed then the ultimate source of Good also had to exist, in the form of a benevolent God. Despite this revelation, I still needed God to manifest Himself in a tangible way. Recalled reading a story in the small pocket-bible that Jesus had healed a demon-possessed man, who was later found to have soundness of mind, sitting peacefully at the feet of Jesus. I desperately prayed and asked the Lord to prove to me that He was real by granting me that same soundness of mind. Allowing me to experience a modern-day miracle and leave this God-forsaken place. While I still had God on the line, I quickly added, "...and if it's not too much to ask, LORD, could you **please have me home by Christmas?**"

Another month passed and still, there was no positive sign leading me to believe that I would be going home anytime soon. I was losing all hope, I stopped praying, and I stopped reading the little Gideon's Bible. Frustrated and desperately angry, I challenged GOD to reveal Himself to me, if He indeed was GOD and if He indeed cared for me the way 'The Word' said He did, then show me, someway, somehow.

One day soon thereafter, I was feeling low, so I went to the Music Room. I came across this old, cracked vinyl LP record and immediately connected. For it was kind of how I felt, cracked, and displaced. I placed it into the record player and was able to fit the needle onto the groove of the last song. It was the only salvageable song in the whole album. It was a very familiar song. I must have heard it a hundred times before, but this time as I listened, it was as if I had heard it for the very first time. The music, the melody, and the lyrics that came out of that old distressed wooden phonograph, with just a mono-solitary speaker sounded like a live orchestra, with an orchestration of angelic hosts. The song seemed to permeate the room and penetrated the inner recesses of my soul. The song was the classic Simon and Garfunkel's:

"Bridge Over Troubled Water." [35]

But it was like Jesus Himself was singing to me ...

TRANSITION

"When you're weary, feeling small
When tears are in your eyes, I will dry them all.
I'm on your side, oh, when times seem rough,
and friends just can't be found...
Like a Bridge over troubled water, I will lay me down
Like a Bridge over troubled water, I will lay me down"

He touched me ... so profoundly, I just stood in that Music Room alone, yet not alone, drinking my tears and crying out to Jesus for doubting his existence. Not only did I know He was real, but I knew somehow, He knew what I was going through, and genuinely cared for me.

In the beginning, I grappled with the chilling realization of evil, a revelation that initially paralyzed me with fear. This very confrontation with darkness would serve as a crucial prelude to the divine intervention awaiting me. It was as if God's Spirit, in His perfect timing, unveiled the truth to me. In that moment, all doubts dissipated, replaced by a profound appreciation for the omnipotent presence of my Creator. The Almighty, in His boundless mercy, reached out and rescued me from the very depths of darkness I had unwittingly plunged myself into. He delivered me from the clutches of my adversaries, beginning with the most formidable foe of all — my own **self**.

December 1975

My brother was a jokester, a real prank artist. I was five, and he was ten years of age, when I recall him putting a towel around his neck one night and going to bed with it on. When I asked him why, he simply responded, "Going flying tonight, wanna go?" At first, I thought he was crazy, but when I saw he just rolled over on his bed and went to sleep, I became very intrigued and quickly woke him up as he had just begun to snore and pleaded, "Yes, I wanna go, please take me with you!" He replied with a chuckle, "You better be awake." The next morning, he was prancing around with the towel still around his neck, bragging about how great it was flying around the Empire State Building, which was lit up all night. I recall getting really upset because he hadn't woken me up.

TRANSITION

This one morning my brother Cano (birth-named Jose aka 'Joe') came to the hospital. I found it strange and asked him, "Cano, what are you doing here so early? Visiting hours isn't until six." He replied with a sly little smirk, "Here, go get your clothes!" handing me a small suitcase. I just stood in total awe with my mouth hanging wide open, frozen, not knowing what to do or say in response. I immediately had a flashback of him with the towel around his neck and thought he was just pulling my leg again. Then he said something that hit me like a lightning bolt, "Well, what are you waiting for?

Don't you want to be home for Christmas?"

It pierced my heart, like multi-electrical surges going through my body causing my hair to rise, and my skin to crawl with goosebumps. I felt like I was on fire. I believe the Spirit was confirming to me that He had heard my prayer request. I wanted so much to share it with my brother, but every time I would even try to open my mouth, I would get all choked up. My brother empathetically remarked, "I understand, Nelson, It's ok. Let's go get your clothes before the doctors change their minds and decide to keep you."

Finally, being set free, to go home and spend the holiday season with the family, just seemed too good to be true. Knowing that this outcome came because of answered prayer made me feel like sharing the good news with the technicians and all the doctors there, but I had to be careful they didn't think I was going over the deep end again. Instead, I took my brother's advice and attempted to conceal this new exhilarating sense of excitement that was just surging through every fiber of my being. My brother was afraid they wouldn't let me go so he hurried me along. Cano drove us back home, to 23 Himrod Street in Brooklyn, the house we were raised in. I just kept thanking God over and over in my mind, drinking in my tears, as I silently prayed, "It's

Christmas Eve, and I'm going to be home with my family. Just in time for Christmas. Forgive me, Father, for ever having doubted you." God was making me whole again, as I was experiencing a sense of peace and joy I could not express in mere words. Through it all, I could almost hear **a small still voice** whispering to my soul,

"Behold, **I AM** 'The Great Physician'
I have not given you a spirit of fear, but of power, of love, and of **a sound mind**." [36]

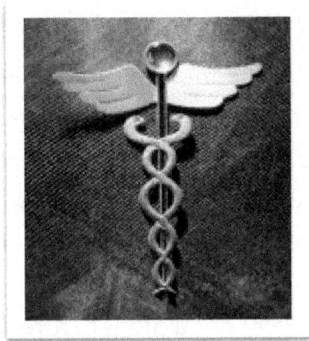

This emblem of the American Medical Association derived from the biblical story of Moses and the serpents in the desert which comes from the Book of Numbers in the Old Testament.
In this story, as the Hebrews wandered in the desert, they faced a plague of venomous snakes sent as a punishment for their rebellion. God instructed Moses to craft a bronze serpent and place it on a pole, (foreshadowing Jesus Christ becoming Sin on the Cross) and those who were bitten by the snakes would look upon it and be healed.

Chapter Eight

Hocus Bogus

After six months of Outpatient Treatment at St. Vincent's they thought I was ready to undertake some responsibility. The doctors agreed to grant me clearance to work in a low-stress part-time position. I was already 18 and didn't feel up to tackling school again. My cousin Louie recommended me for a job working with him at Eagle Electric. Louie acted more like another big brother than just a cousin. Thus, to the envy of my other cousins, I honored him with the title "Best" cousin. He was trigueno (dark-skinned), very athletic, and was always taking me under his wing trying to show me how to play B-Ball, as well as other more rugged sports like football. Lending me his two-sizes-too-large shoulder pads, and a helmet too big for my head. Much of his noble efforts to help mold me into some sports jock, never really took. Apparently, I was gifted with more cranial capacity than physical assertiveness.

Eagle Electric was a factory in Queens that manufactured electric sockets. My duties required me to assist my cousin in retrieving barrels of plastic receptacles and lifting them onto tables for women to sort out. It wasn't too hard, with my "Best" cousin looking out for me, I was able to eventually work full-time for about a year.

I became bored and disillusioned once again, and *as a sow returned to the mud and a dog to its vomit.* The fear of God dwindled in me, and I was back to my boozing and drug-inducing ways. Around that same time, I became entranced by the mysterious allure of the occult, exploring the realm of witchcraft. Initially dismissing it as benign "White Witchcraft," I soon realized that, regardless of the label, the devil recognizes no boundaries—it's all malevolent. Creating a makeshift altar on my dresser, I engaged in the ritual of lighting candles and offering prayers to the false deities outlined in their witch's handbook. Intriguingly, these same entities were associated with the Catholic Church during their communion, an association revealed by the Holy Spirit as part of what they termed their blasphemous "Black Mass." This revelation exposed a dark aspect of their communion ceremony, linking it to a practice within the Catholic Church. *(see Chapter 4)*

The truly frightening aspect unfolded when I started receiving everything I wished for—money, sex, free drugs—but it all came at a grave cost, *for the wages of sin is death.* It reminded me of the wisdom in Psalm 23, the same passage my kind earth angel from the hospital had urged me to read. The opening verse, "The LORD is my Shepherd; I Shall Not Want!" struck a chord. It's a lesson about fleshly desire, understanding that God knows precisely what we need, and wisdom guides us to find contentment in that knowledge. It was like opening Pandora's Box. I had opened a portal to the gates of hell and had invited all kinds of demonic activity to wreak havoc upon my life, filling me with utter fear and torment. I became so afraid and paranoid that I would not leave my house for any reason. With each attempt to summon my courage, a chilling obstacle stood in my path. Out of nowhere, barking dogs materialized, their snarling echoes penetrated the air fueling my trepidation. Their aggressive pursuit created an atmosphere of terror and hindered any progress I sought to make.

As if the canine menace wasn't enough, the people around me added to my nightmarish disquietude, with contorted unnerving grins, their eyes glimmering with an unsettling awareness of pure evil. It was as if they possessed a profound understanding *of my* thoughts and intentions, their sinister smiles artificially glued to their faces. Their eerie presence sending shivers down my spine. My aunt "Titi" Gladys discovered the book on White Witchcraft, which I had ordered via some magazine, on my dresser. I guess she was possibly looking for my hidden stash and found the book instead. She confronted me because, after all, I was officially living in her house, where my mom was renting out the upstairs apartment. I fessed up, gave up the drugs I had stashed, and asked her forgiveness and her help. So, my aunt stepped up and went on a mission to help me, by taking me to speak with her Priest at St. Theresa's. After reciting about 25 Our Fathers and 25 Hail Mary's, my aunt saw it hardly phased me. She upped her game, and the following weekend took me to a place called "El Centro" (The Centre). It was another kind of church, where they congregated at night; Titi falsely advised me they might be more capable of helping me in my situation. They practiced a different form of Catholicism called "Santeria" where they called out to the saints to intervene. They closed the doors and warned us not to leave once they started. Women were lighting smelly cigars and blowing the smoke into the air and into our faces. They began speaking in lower decibels sounding more like men. A man dressed all in white and a red sash began yelling out names I didn't recognize. He claimed they were the names of the saints translated into African dialect. By the time we left that cold smoke-filled creep show, I felt like I had just experienced a real-life horror movie in the making. What really scared the bejesus out of me was the uncanny realization that although it wasn't a movie, somehow, I landed the starring role.

The last couple of years were like a blur attempting to re-engage and re-enter society. I was too heavily medicated and still falling into abusing alcohol, which sure enough didn't help the process.

Reset going into 1978 with a new outlook, and a new job, worked as a messenger for a graphic arts firm called Line & Tone Associates, across Bryant Park and The New York Public Library in mid-Manhattan. My boss, a warm sensitive Jewish man, by the name of Henry Mayer took me under his wing, mentored and trained me as a Darkroom tech, taking and developing photostatic copies.

In the Fall I registered for Night School to begin working towards obtaining my G.E.D., where I met this beautiful Latina with jet-black hair in my class by the name of Sonia. We hit it off really well and after just a couple of months, we decided to shack up and rent an apartment together. We celebrated the holiday season and went into the New Year of '79 thinking we could live off love. Although the illusion didn't even last a year. We graduated from Night School, and both got our Equivalency Diplomas.

Shortly after the Summer Sonia's first love came back from the Marine Corps and re-claimed her. Just as quickly as she had come into my life she slipped out, running off and marrying him. Leaving me broken-hearted I resumed hanging out with my partners-in-crime, relapsing back into senselessly numbing my brain with cocaine.

A year transpired, and the apartment which started as a love nest became just another sleazy drug infested hang-out. One night I was awoken from a drunken stupor to hear someone or something breaking down my kitchen door. For a minute I thought it was '5-O' busting through with a battering ram, but two leaps later it was on top of me.

TRANSITION

I couldn't see what it was in the dark, and I felt as if I had been hit by lightning. I was paralyzed by an invisible, electrical force field powered by fear. I couldn't yell, couldn't move, or breathe... it was like being snuffed out by some demonic hitman. As I found myself engulfed in utter darkness, an overwhelming sense of dread washed over me. I was on the precipice of an unimaginable terror, fully aware that I was being mercilessly pulled down into the depths of what felt like an infernal abyss. The weight of the situation pressed upon me, suffocating any flicker of hope or respite. The horrific realization of my impending fate intensified my fear, as I grappled with the chilling notion that I was being consumed by the very essence of hell itself.

I was ready to pass out when self-preservation kicked in, and in a last desperate attempt, through gritted teeth, was somehow able to get out **"Jesus!"** The dark apparition that felt like a 200-pound hound from hell immediately released me. Turning prostrate onto my belly on that urine-reeking mattress, I began crying out to God for forgiveness faced-down in a praying hysteria until daybreak. God had given me a glimpse of the dark side, putting a literal fear of Himself into every fiber of my being. Since I wasn't too interested in seeking His love, He gave me a little taste of His wrath instead, and so well deserved.

I walked aimlessly from the Brooklyn borderline of Ridgewood into Queens, muttering to myself like one of those crazy people you avoid in the streets of NYC. With a pressing need to chart a new path, I had a lot to figure out. It was evident that I had to make a recourse and break free from the negative element which was engulfing me in the Hood. Desperation began setting in, as I felt the urgency to shift gears, enter into survival mode and reclaim my life. Time seemed to lapse as I must have walked countless miles right into a commercial shopping district.

Then GOD literally gave me a sign, as well as an answer to all my inquiries. Also revealing a sense of humor during all the insanity. I broke out in nervous laughter, as I noticed a big billboard looming up at me from across the main avenue.

TRANSITION

The sign seemed to satirically shout...

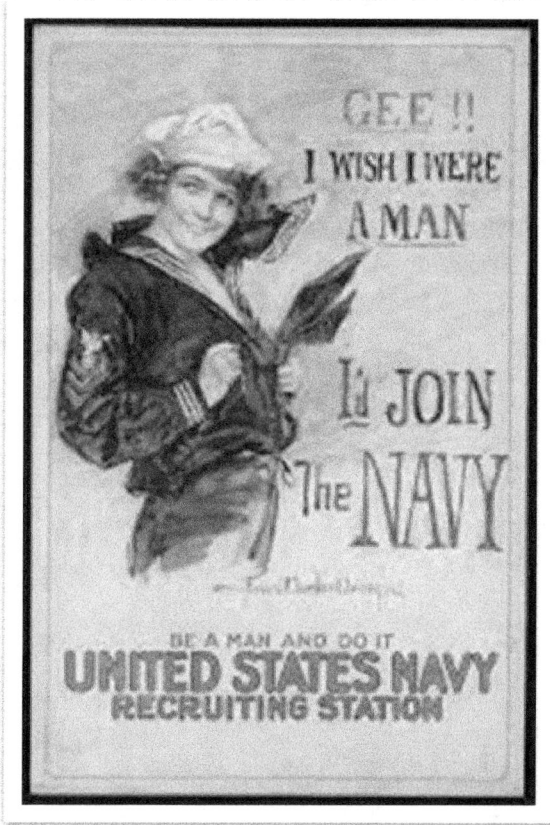

"ATTENTION!"

Chapter Nine

In The Navy

To this day, I thank GOD for that demon; the catalyst which made me join the Navy. Although I didn't want to go during the Winter and requested to join via the Delayed Entry Program. My recruiter explained I would have to be inducted immediately for me to attain and secure my guaranteed "A-School." I was granted the privilege of spending Thanksgiving with the family. The following week I was sworn in and inducted into the Navy and immediately shipped out to Great Lakes Naval Training Command in Illinois. At 22 years of age, in hopes of a reset, I chose not to divulge anything pertaining to my medical history or my drug use, fearing rejection. I was determined to leave the neighborhood at any cost. In His infinite wisdom, God intervened, granting me the opportunity to join the Navy and avoid the premature fate that had befallen many of my associates. Thus, I embarked on my journey to Great Lakes, Illinois, for basic training, commonly referred to as 'Boot Camp.

I discovered leadership qualities in me I didn't even know I had when they placed me in charge of five other men in my squad. We were like the Wild Bunch, the Dirty Dozen, and the Devil's Brigade all rolled up into one unit. Half of our company were Yankees from the northeast, and the other half might as well have been Confederates from the south. In the beginning, we were all constantly fighting and having our own private civil war. By the time our Company Commander Chief Hidalgo got through with us, we became one well-oiled greased machine. Chief Hidalgo was from the Philippines, and no more than five feet tall. We thought we had all been shanghaied by the Japanese Navy when he so tenderly woke us up that first frosty morning, "Get up, Get up, you SOB's!" We instantly bonded. The "Lollipop Guild"[37] quickly came to mind, as he was comparably short in stature and just as tough. He would not settle for anything less but excellence. That's exactly what it took to whip us all into tip-top shape and made us pull together as one unit.

It was a cold winter there that year. The wind was biting at our noses and fingertips. The sky was emptied of all life. It was an Antarctic wind. Whiteout - blinded by the snow, and the sun shining off it. Dropping as low as 40 below one morning, when they classified it "Code Blue." We were allowed to march with our gloved hands in our pockets to avoid hypothermia. They even bypassed the smokehouse that day, afraid the vomit might freeze in our mouths. The training protocol routinely calls to douse us with tear gas and order us to take off our gas masks and recite the 1st General Order - "I will not quit my post until properly relieved-SIR!"

I began reading my Gideon's mini-pocket New Testament that the faithful woman of God had given me when I was at St. Vincent's Hospital. I would wait till I heard "Lights Out!" at 2100 hours. Going underneath my issued gray wool blanket, I discreetly turned on my flashlight and browsed through it. I became inspired to attend Sunday Service one morning, assuming it was a Catholic Mass. When I arrived at the Navy drill hall, I expected to see a Priest dressed in their usual ritualistic robe. I was surprised to discover an Officer, who was a Chaplain, conducting worship. Men were singing and raising their arms up to God in surrender, and once again I sensed the Holy Spirit, but this time with a lot more intensity. I felt like I had just stepped into the *Twilight Zone*.

I knew this wasn't a Catholic Mass, but I was glued to the seat, and I just couldn't move. There was such a tugging at my heart that I was paralyzed with apprehension. I didn't understand what was happening to me. I felt an intense heat rising from the nape of my neck onto my head. I was fighting back the tears when one of the men seated behind me placed his hand on my shoulder and proceeded to say, "It's alright man, let it go!" When I looked to see who it was, it just happened to be a co-sailor from my company, another Newyorican homeboy from the Bronx named Negron. The dam broke as my soul began to cry out. I was immediately hugged by him and the surrounding men, as the Protestant Chaplain began to pray for me. What a release of old pent-up emotions. Never sensed anything like that before. Intrigued to experience more of that refreshing sense of uninhibited freedom, I couldn't wait to graduate from Boot Camp to attend more of those powerful Protestant Services. I was so brainwashed by the ideological supremacy of the Catholic Church claiming to be "the only true and Apostolic Church" that I almost felt guilty for having attended a Protestant service. Although I was strongly compelled by the Holy Spirit to attend services at The First Baptist Church of Millington, and eventually, I was baptized again, after having graduated from Boot Camp. Never felt like my initial infant baptism counted, after all, I couldn't even remember the occasion. This time I was dressed in a white robe and literally dunked in total immersion of water. It was so invigorating, just like the Bible depicted, sensing rivers of "Living Water" washing, purging, and cleansing me. Being the good Catholic that I was, and coming from many years of habitual pre-conditioning, I still couldn't help but do the sign of the cross just before getting dunked by the Minister. When asked by the other converts why I did the sign of the cross, I quickly responded, "Last Rites."

After winning most of the competitive flags we graduated with honors being the top company graduating from Boot Camp that year. I had tried out for the SEALS, while in Boot Camp, but washed out during the initial swimming phase. One had to pass an underwater obstacle course, and out of 200 participants, only about 20 finished successfully. It ended with frogmen dragging me out of the testing pool after I had swallowed and breathed water. I'm not ashamed to admit I'm not Aquaman or even half a merman.

They were immediately shipped off to Naval Special Warfare Center in Coronado, California: The Navy SEAL's official hell's beach for the commencement of their infamous "**Hell~Week**[1]": Testing physical endurance, mental toughness, pain and cold tolerance, teamwork, attitude, and your ability to perform work under high physical and mental stress, and sleep deprivation. Above all, it tests determination and desire.

---

1.   https://navyseals.com/nsw/hell-week-0/

On average, only 20 to 25 percent of SEAL candidates make it through Hell Week, the toughest training in the U.S. Military. It is often the greatest achievement of their lives, and with it comes the realization that they can do 20 times more than they ever thought possible. It is a defining moment that they reach back to when in combat. Knowing that they will never, ever quit, or let a teammate down.

I went on to 'A' School stationed at a Naval Air Base in Millington, Tennessee. I ran in their Track Team because I could. Being a Long-Distance runner was my specialty back in Automotive High, where I was relieved not to have to be concerned about some tedious sport where the main object was to catch, carry, hit, or run after a ball, which I never had a knack for. Now when I found out that there was a Boxing Team on this Naval Base, I joined. I was always intrigued by the sport of Boxing, where all I would have to learn to do is hit and take a hit.

I remember back in the day when I would visit my mother's only brother, Uncle Willie in the LES of Manhattan's prestigious projects. His wife, my beautiful black Puerto Rican Aunt Carmen, nicknamed "Cambu" would usually have a holiday dinner waiting for us, especially around Christmas. Latino soul food consisted of Arroz con glandules (Yellow Rice with Pigeon Peas), Pasteles, and a big pork roast or "Penir."

I would be playing with my cousins in their room while the adults conversed in their native tongue, drinking some festive Caribbean coconut eggnog, "Coquito" and chowing down in the kitchen. While my Uncle Willie played his classic "Navidad" 78/RPM 10-inch vintage vinyl on his big RCA console record player. My cousin Luis, whose close circle of friends had him nick-named "Black Louie", to help distinguish him from the other Louies in the neighborhood. He was just a couple of years older and was a natural athlete.

I was about 11, when he dug out of his closet a couple of aged musty pair of brown leather boxing gloves. He was supposedly going to teach me how to box. Enthusiastically, my cousin began donning his gloves, while my younger cousin Carlos helped me with mine. He told me to put my dukes up, while Carlos began snickering and made the sound of the bell.

I just stood there dumbfounded hearing my cousin Louie ring out his warning, "Put 'em up, put 'em up, put your dukes up, cause here I come!" As he started doing the "Ali Shuffle" and showing off his fancy footwork. I began trying to mimic him, but as I was focusing on his feet, he gave me a straight right hand hitting me square on my mug. I stood there for a second, resembling a cartoon, trying to figure out what had just happened, then tottering and falling face down onto my cousin's bed. "TKO!" They yelled as I just lay there on the bed face down trying to muster some courage to get back up but decided it would probably be safer to stand down, stay down, and just play dead.

Ever since, I vowed to learn the sport of Boxing. The Navy Boxing Team was that glorious opportunity to learn it properly by the Navy's standards and learn it well. After finishing BEEP (Basic Electricity and Electronics Preliminary) School, I volunteered for *H.A.R.P.* Duty: *Hometown Assistance Recruiting Program (HARP): allows Sailors to report to the nearest Recruiting Station to their hometowns for 12 days to their Recruiters by relating their Navy experiences to their peers.*

Advanced Electronics Program

It was an extensive program in which they attempted to fit 2 years of advanced electronics training into six months. Being the overachiever that I was, I was doubling up the workload and taking two manuals instead of just one. Whatever you took home with you to study, you were expected to know fully by the next day. "Lights Out!" was at 2100 hrs. I would use my flashlight to comb through the manual till about 1 am. I was like a madman on a mission to attain my AX specialty with my 1st chevron, as I would rank up to Petty Officer 3rd Class. I would then be tested the following day on each manual, and passing was nothing less than 100%. You were expected to ace every test.

Once you passed the written test, then you would be tested manually on the actual circuitry. After doing it for two months, took two manuals to my barracks, and studied them all night. To be tested the next day, after maybe just a couple of hours of sleep, and having to ace both tests, eventually took its toll on me.

Entering April 1981, on **Good Friday**, my mind inevitably blew a fuse. The blinking lights on most of the complex circuits I was being tested on must have tripped something in my brain's circuitry to short circuit. That and not to mention all the stress and duress I placed on myself must have caused a great strain on my brain. All these stressors combined may have contributed highly to my central nervous system shutting down and thus causing a seizure. Although now I strongly believe when I experienced the seizure, I may have been going through some early process of deliverance from demonic oppression.

At the Naval Hospital, I was stripped of all my clothing and told to put on one of their skimpy hospital gowns. When they asked me to take off the rosary beads, I always wore, I hesitated and told them that they belonged to my grandmother who had it blessed for me. They insisted I remove it from around my neck, but when I went to do so I was compelled to kiss the crucifix like I must have done a million times before. But this time something amazing happened, as I closed my eyes and kissed it. I envisioned Christ on the Cross, and it all happened in a blink of an eye. It was drummed into my head by nuns and priests for so many previous years during Religious Instructions and Catholic Mass, but it never took. I couldn't figure out in my finite little mind how God in His infinite wisdom, holy and righteous would come in the form of a broken man two thousand years ago and die for me. It just wouldn't register. Why me? He didn't know me then, or did He? It took for me to get a glimpse of him on the cross for it to finally sink in... from my head to my heart. Hitting me like a thunderbolt, I grabbed the nearest tech, and with tears rolling down my eyes, I cried out, "He died for me!"

They proceeded to escort me to the Quiet Room, as I kept getting glimpses of Christ on the Cross. I tried to convince them that I wasn't crazy. That I had a vision of Jesus, as the technicians made a gesture to place me into the 10 by 20 room, and with a little struggle, they finally did. It had nothing but a cold bare plastic-coated mattress on the floor, and a very small wire-mesh window letting minimal sunlight into that cold dark room.

It was "Good Friday", and they had explained to me that the Medical Officer had already left for the day, and he wouldn't be back on duty until the following Monday. They didn't know what to do with me, so military protocol required I be locked in a controlled environment. I spent the entire weekend in isolation, **But GOD** met me there.

I was **crucified with Christ on Friday.** While it's impossible for me to fully grasp the entirety of the merciless agonizing pain and humiliation that Christ must have endured for me on that rugged cross. I was granted a glimpse, just a mere inkling, but a fraction of the true depth of Christ's suffering. His sacrifice, His immense love... as I meditated on how my rebellious ways, and all of my selfish fleshly pursuits played a part in placing Him on that horrid cross.

All day, into the night, and on Saturday (the Sabbath) the Spirit brought to memory the illicit, hateful, malicious sins in my life: the many times I disrespected my mother, as well as my grandmother, and broke their hearts as well as God's. The numerous times I had brought pain to anyone who tried to befriend me, lied, connived, betrayed and hurt those closest to me. Christ revealed to me by His Spirit that He had taken all those sins, past, present, as well as any future sins, which I had not yet committed, and pinned them all to that hellish **Cross at Calvary.** Despite all my failures, Christ's faithful love reached beyond my understanding, encompassing even the depths of my brokenness.

NELSON COLÓN

Then came Sunday...
Crying may endure for a night, but joy comes in the morning!
[38] and my soul seemed to resurrect with the **Living Christ.**

I found myself, or shall I say they found me dancing stark naked as a jaybird, as the warm sun penetrated that wire-mesh window lighting up the room. There came such a release from so much excess baggage I was carrying around, such an elated feeling of uninhibited freedom, such an overwhelming sensation of,

Joy inexpressible and full of glory! [39]

I really couldn't explain it. All I know, I was hopelessly lost, until my faithful Heavenly Father found me. Even though my deep spiritual experiences in the Navy were so traumatic, to a certain extent, they were the most important first steps on the incredible journey of my eventual spiritual awakening. I felt like a newborn baby. Sensing the Holy Spirit endowing me with rivers of joy.

... for the Joy of the Lord is your strength.

As the Spirit of the risen Christ resonated deep within my soul, I heard that small still, yet strong reassuring voice, ...

"Rejoice and do not despair,
For **I** have not called you into man's army.
I AM calling you into **Mine!"**

BAM-Incorporated
Joined forces with
7BridgestoRecovery.org

Bringing food & supplies
"Blankets & Bibles"
Under the Pro-Vision Program
to the Homeless in the ATL-Metro area.
Kingdom Minds Advancing, Inc.
2019

Chapter Ten

Back In the Hood

Being "Honorably Discharged" carried no honor. The Navy, hypocritically, failed to honor me with medical benefits despite my discharge being for a medical condition. I ventured out of Brooklyn to the Navy, envisioning it as the gateway to the wider world. "Not just a job, but an adventure!" they promised. Inadvertently, my mental fortitude crumbled, a result of the extensive stress and duress imposed by their 'advanced training,' robbing me of the ability to persevere. They disavowed any responsibility for the seizure, branding my DD214 with "Personality Disorder," washing their hands of me and thrusting me back to the slums. They had no inkling of the true disorder which was still within my being.

Returning home felt like a confrontation with the Angel of Death. The comrades of my youth succumbed to the repercussions of their reckless lifestyles. Jimmy, my brother-in-law, fell to Hepatitis. Lucky and Ray, brothers in life and death, succumbed to the ruthless grip of AIDS, two weeks apart. Carlos, my supposed best friend who unwittingly initiated me into hardcore

drugs, outlived them all. Yet, he too eventually succumbed to the monster several years later.

My good old friends, when they were alive, were just thrilled to have me back, as they passed around the wine bottle along with a lit joint, while I attempted to share the vision I had of Jesus on the Cross. Carlos would just grin nonchalantly saying, "It was just a flashback from that Acid punch. Come on Nelson, you saved? You are no different from the rest of us." His brothers Ray and Lucky would just shake their heads and laugh in harmonious mockery.

They were right, I was no different from any of them, yet GOD chose to reveal Himself to me. Why me? The more I tried to win my friends over, the less I seemed to get through, they were weakening me. It was just a matter of time before I would begin self-medicating, waking up in dirty tenement halls, shivering and detoxing on the street corners of Brooklyn again. The LORD did warn me in His Word, *"Bad company corrupts good morals!"* The company I kept was indeed only taking me down an all too familiar road.

TRANSITION

---

1. https://www.youtube.com/watch?v=zCT2oclzxe0

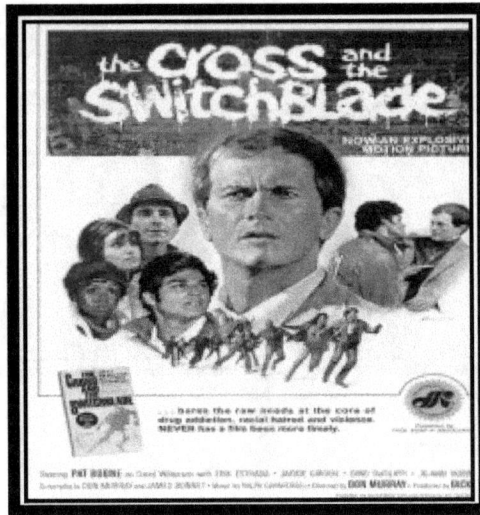

I moved out from Bushwick, across the tracks to Fort Hamilton. Became a courier, delivering stocks and bonds throughout the Wall Street area, and got married to a lower East-Side native, like me.

We started to visit churches throughout Downtown Brooklyn, looking for a place where we could connect and grow with others who knew and loved Jesus; where we could learn more about Him, and live a life where joy and peace are prevalent. Joy and peace were rarities in my life until this point. The Brooklyn Tabernacle Church then became our home. I became an Usher. She was gifted with a voice, so she joined the Choir. Pastor Jim Cymbala proved to be a tremendous mentor and teacher. Eventually, I became so involved with the church that I even started doing evangelism throughout the streets of Brooklyn. Growing up, street evangelists always seemed so angry, yelling about the wrath of God, the corruption of our nation, etc. This was different, it was compassionate.

Jesus stated He came for the sick, and that the Heart of God is mercy.

On a special occasion we went out with Nicky Cruz, a former South Brooklyn gangster made famous by *"The Cross and The Switchblade,"* a book written by a local pastor David Wilkerson.[40] It was later made into a major motion picture, starring Pat Boone and Erik Estrada. Most of our street ministry went to the infamous Alphabet City, on Avenues A through D in the Lower East Side. We set up some speakers with the sound system in a public park and blared some soft, but strongly anointed worship music from Brooklyn Tabernacle Choir which set the atmosphere. While Nicky Cruz grabbed the mic, and like a madman jumped on a stone checkerboard table, knocking off the dominos...

His voice thundered, as if there was a storm in his spirit, shouting in his broken Spanglish accent, "Mira mi Gente, my people, we are here on a mission.

NELSON COLÓN

We're gonna have a spiritual **rrrumble** here tonight...
Gonna bring down all these principalities and powers and take over
this devil's territory ...
We take authority, right now, in the name of **JESUS!**"
Parks were infested with prostitution and drugs.
Junkies and women on the streets would just come up crying, willingly
surrendering their drugs and paraphernalia.
Throwing their stuff as well as themselves
on concrete grounds.

Even the cops were amazed!

I instantly fell in love with street ministry.

"For life has to fight for the right to live."

I was privileged to be called to be one of **God's agents of reconciliation**, not afraid to go into the front lines and be the "Hands and Feet" of Jesus, reaching out and sharing the Love of the Living Christ. I used to have two jobs in the Wall Street area, working as a messenger during the day, and then working in the banks as a watchman at night. I worked at both gigs through different agencies that didn't offer any benefits. I just barely made $250 per week, and that was the total from both jobs. I was also in training for the New York City Marathon and used to run during my lunch break. I also ran at night to get in my ten to fifteen miles for the day. But the Lord came through right on time as my wife became pregnant with my first-born Nethaniel.

I was called for a position I had applied for as a Hospital Security-Police in a private hospital. Lutheran Medical Center was conveniently located near us in the Bay Ridge area of Brooklyn. They paid very well, double, and then some, exceedingly more than what I was doing with the other two jobs put together. I was able to join the Patrolmen's Benevolent Association which had great benefits. When our son Nethaniel came into the world, they covered everything. We called him our "Miracle Baby" because his mother almost miscarried him at 4 months and was restricted to bed rest for the remainder of her pregnancy.

One year the hospital staff members, the orderlies, the maintenance people, and every worker who belonged to the hospital's Union 1199 went on strike, and we in charge of security and maintaining the peace throughout the hospital grounds had to work 12 to 16-hour shifts. I mainly worked the evening shifts back-to-back with the graveyard shifts. I hardly saw my wife. I would come home to relieve her as she went to her city job in the fashion district, and I would then tend to Nethaniel who was just a toddler. Many times, my dear Mama would take the train all the way from the other side of Brooklyn to help me watch and care for her grandson, as I attempted to catch some Zs. Father GOD, "Papa Dios" as my mom reared us up to call Him, granted me the divine appointment to help usher her into His Kingdom.

One evening after a dinner she had lovingly prepared, during our conversation I respectfully asked her permission to veer off the frivolous talk and present to her a seriously deep question. After she acknowledged and agreed, I proceeded to ask her, "Mami, God forbid it, but if you would die tonight. Do you know where your spirit would go?" After a long pause, she proceeded to tell me how she felt she was a good mother, sacrificing herself for us as a sole parent, doing the best she knew how to provide for us... and on she went as I allowed her to continue with her self-promotion trying to convince me, as well as herself, that she was a good enough person who hoped to make it into Heaven. I then asked her if I could show her in the Bible where it is written how she can be truly assured of her salvation. She complied, "Si Mijo, Como no!" [41]

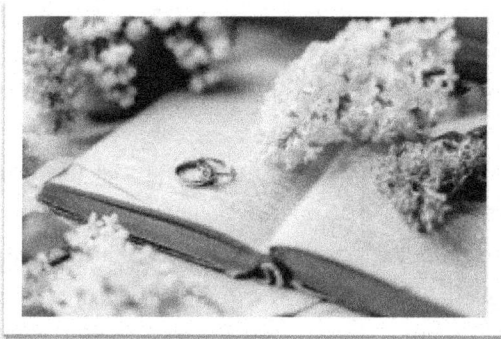

I broke out the "Big Guns" and handed her a "Sagrada Biblia" I had bought her. She was pleasantly surprised and yet intrigued as to why I would purchase such an elaborate gift for her. It was a Bible translated into her native language. I then proceeded to show her in the sacred Word that stated that ***there is none righteous;*** *For all have sinned and fallen short,* to help her conclude that it's not about our good works, but that we're **all** in dire need of the Savior. Afterward, I went to the

Book of Romans / Chapter 10: verses 9 and 10 - *If you declare with your mouth, "Jesus is Lord," and believe in your heart that God raised him from the dead, you will be saved. For it is with your heart that you believe and are justified, and it is with your mouth that you profess your faith and are saved.*

I recited the scripture verses in Spanish, as the Spirit directed me, and her spiritual eyes were opened. My mom began crying, as she experienced the presence of the Holy Spirit, possibly for the first time. I consoled her and led her in prayer to receive Jesus as her personal

LORD, as well as Savior.   My mama finally met and married the perfect Groom that day. The One that could truly love her forever. She brought me into this world, and GOD blessed me with the glorious opportunity and honor to introduce her to Jesus. Her true Husbandman.

After four years of marriage, my wife and I became strangers. We inevitably drifted apart, not having time for each other, or for church. We would hardly speak, too busy for conversation, just saying hi and bye as we passed the baton. I came home one morning after my graveyard shift, just to discover that she had packed up her stuff, as well as the baby, and gone off on one of her escapades to Puerto Rico. About a month later she finally came back home. "Had fun?" I facetiously inquired. "I want a divorce!" she vindictively replied. Insult added to Injury. My festering wounds opened, as I just slumped, dumbfounded, and devastated, further into my living room chair like a wounded animal, longing to be put out of its misery with the final kill shot.

From where we resided, at 62nd street and third, I walked up to 5th avenue, the shopping district. As I continued to walk the cleanliness of the town declined. Fewer shoppers, more drug dealers. Ghetto decline, drug dealers, thick rope chains and tattoos on their necks, bandanas, leather jackets, new designer jeans, ball caps, and Yankee ball caps. In the 1970s black and yellow were the gang colors for Black Stone Nation in Bed-Stuy; on my side of the neighborhood (right across Broadway) in the Bushwick zone where we were predominantly Latino. My gang, 'Homicide Laws' colors bled Red on Black. We knew when people were in some gang because they were always parading their colors, especially on their turf, but in the 80s gangsters became more inconspicuous.

They didn't have to fly any colors for you to know they were somehow connected; the drug dealers were cruising around in their Corvettes and Camaros while they had their runners hanging out dispersing their drugs, yet they dressed better than those who were just hanging out getting high. Everyone was walking out of the pawnshop in a rush to get their fix. I became possessed, like a man on a mission, a suicide mission. I followed suit, pawned my wedding band, and after four years of being clean, I chose to relapse. Joining the ranks of the walking dead once again, taking the funds I acquired from having sold the ring I copped my drugs of preference, cocaine, and heroin. As I did the drugs in the back of my car, I felt the Holy Spirit lift off me. The most dreadful sense of hopelessness and deep despair took its place, as my heart just seemed to plummet back into the depths of hell. I knew I had just grieved God's Holy Spirit, with serious repercussions and consequences to follow.

The Bible speaks of a man whose house was swept clean, symbolizing his soul, and that a demon that was cast out would come back, as the man consciously chose to fall back into practicing sin, giving access to that demon that had left, which would come back with seven demons worse than himself.[42] Things did get worse, I got worse and did things that I am still terribly ashamed of even to this day. I would cook the cocaine with the heroin, praying that I would O.D. As I infused the searing elixir into my veins, I found myself engaged in a lament, embittered and seething, directing my ire towards the Divine. With each fiery drop of poison coursing through my bloodstream, I vocalized my self-curses, a futile attempt in the unburdening of the soul, my indignation vented upon the heavens. In this intimate communion with the substance, I wrestled with the profound complexity of my existence, torn between the agony of the present and the deep turmoil of my faith, like a soul adrift in a turbulent sea of utter despair.

Can't even remember how many times I overdosed, waking up in an emergency room getting my stomach pumped, and being made to chug-a-lug liquid charcoal. But God with His stubborn love and yes, amazing grace, would still wake me up the next day. After coming out of a self-induced coma, I would rush to get to work, unshaven, unshowered, and standing at my post, often sweating profusely through my uniform. However, this routine didn't last long, as I was immediately brought before the Director of Security, Mr. Kiernan, a retired Detective, accompanied by an executive from the hospital administration. The union couldn't do a thing to keep them from terminating me. Inevitably I hit rock bottom, and in utter desperation, I asked to speak to my Pastor Jim Cymbala from Brooklyn Tabernacle and confessed, "Pastor I need help!" He and his Co-Pastor Anthony Impaglia conferred and in turn referred me straight to Teen Challenge. There I was finally able to get the help and support I needed. I remember the whole team of leaders and counselors praying over me that first night. I felt such a warmth covering me like a comforter, no wonder why Jesus referred to the 3rd Person of the Trinity as that. I slept like a baby and didn't even go through any withdrawals. The surging tide of GOD's grace came breaking through, washing over me, and proving once again that it was indeed greater than all my sinful folly could ever be.

Looking back, I realize that my experience of taking a drop down into that dark abyss after my first encounter with the Light is not entirely unusual for a person in my position at the time. We read that King David in the Bible was anointed King as a young man, yet he spent many years after that being hunted in the wilderness before he received his Crown. This seems to be a natural progression on many spiritual journeys. Jesus received the Holy Spirit after John baptized him in the Jordan river and after that, he immediately found himself in the desert being tempted by satan. So, if you encounter Jesus on your personal journey and afterward experience a descent back into the abyss, don't despair – the bright light of Day is not far off! If the Good Lord wakes you up yet another day, I can assuredly say,

"GOD still has a purpose for your life!"

Chapter Eleven

Crossroads of Convictions

<u>**November 1988**</u>

I was determined to hang on to my spiritual progress this time, and not relinquish it the same way I had after my Medical Discharge from the Navy. After Teen Challenge, all clean and restored, I really didn't feel very secure staying in New York. I was afraid that I might fall back into my old self-destructive escapades. By 1988, I left the states altogether and relocated to my parent's native island, Puerto Rico. I lived out there in the metropolitan area of San Juan, working Security night shifts at El San Juan Hotel and Casino. I bought a Hotdog Stand and sold hotdogs, hamburgers, and tropical fruit drinks during the day by Isla Verde's Beaches. Loved it out there, didn't even care if I sold anything. I would just take my beach lounge chair, take in some rays, and breathe in the good salt air.

Was even able to land a good-paying job with a very well-known newspaper in the Island *El Vocero*, infamous for its graphic front-page photos. One evening when I was watching the front desk, where you would watch the monitors and buzz people into the facility, I allowed access to two individuals, Mr. Mangual, in charge of interviewing and writing articles about rising new talents in Puerto Rico. Came in and introduced me to Marc Anthony, who at the time was still an unknown. *"Mira, este es un–New Yorican como tú!"*[43] He blurted out to me, as Marc Anthony shook my hand and gave me one of the record albums that he was carrying underneath his other arm. I still have the album, it's a white-covered album with a 45" Big Vinyl Disco record and his picture on the cover, Marc 'The Rebel" Anthony printed on it. If I had any clue that he was going to become such a big "Star", I would have had him sign the album and take a pic with me, although come to think of it, we didn't have cell phones those days to take selfies with. This meeting did remind me later that we should always be prepared for unusual blessings that may come our way; who knows? I might have taken Marc Anthony's autograph and sold it later for thousands of dollars.

Time went on as time does, and because I did not experience any real growth in my spiritual walk the slow creeping darkness caught up with me again. After a couple of years, I began drinking and inevitably using again. I picked up a DUI and had to sell my classic '74 Camaro to make restitution. I sold my Hotdog Stand, quit my job with *El Vocero*, and moved back to the states. So much for my *Isla Del Encanto* (Enchanted Island) experience. Not wanting to give in to defeat and end up back in New York, in 1990 I relocated to Orlando, where my sister Lilly paved the way for me to follow. It turned out to be a positive move. I went back to school, while I worked the graveyard shift as a Security/Night Manager at the Omni Hotel.

Strategically situated right across from what was the Omni Centro-Plex Sports Arena. Felt like a celebrity, hanging out with the players of the fresh new extension basketball team, the Orlando Magic.

TRANSITION

Deciding to take up a trade and break into the medical field, for a change of pace. Becoming an x-ray tech, I was able to leave my night position and began working 12-hour shifts at various Walk-In Clinics throughout Orlando. Took up Kung-Fu and Tai-Chi for three years, to give me some recreational outlet for my pent-up anger issues, as well as practice some self-control. Even joined another church in Central Florida by the name of Faith Assembly. I Sang in the choir and stirred up those creative communication gifts and talents within me by also partaking in plays with the Drama Team.

One great play I auditioned for was *Heaven's Gates and Hell's Flames*, where I was called back for the lead role of satan. Go Figure! They set up a very professional stage and put me into a costume with startling realistic make-up, although I ended up looking more like Gene Simmons of the Kings in Satan's Service (KISS). The drama turned out to be such a success that at the end of the first show, young people were running to the altar. Pastor Stephens extended the show for the entire week and asked me to stay after one of the presentations, while I was helping to pray over those who had answered the altar call. Maybe my performance was too overwhelmingly convincing, so much so that he wanted me to stay and get prayed over as well.

As I studied my lines, I asked GOD to help me ad-lib and capture the evil mindset of the enemy's role. I did so well that pastors and other members of the Drama Team began looking at me kind of strangely, and remarked, "You looked like you were enjoying that a little bit too much, Nelson." I would come up in a cloud of smoke and appear on stage improvising, "I smell a preacher's kid, I just love preacher's kids ...", smacking my lips and sticking out my tongue. They had the decibels on my mic for the sound of my voice set so low, that I even scared myself. That was back in 1992, and since it turned out to be such a great outreaching extravaganza, they are still doing it every Halloween to

145

this day. Yes, I must admit to being a little proud of that achievement, although I try not to give myself too many accolades for it, especially since I was portraying the enemy. But it was solely GOD's anointing upon my performance that brought the conviction upon so many. So, the glory completely goes to Him!

I have always been somewhat of a ham for attention, and so around that same time, I even did a little background "Extra" work and played a policeman in *Passenger 57*. Having met and had the privilege of enjoying lunch with Wesley Snipes, and Tom Sizemore. I was also called to play a Journalist in *Contact* with Jodie Foster and Matthew McConaughey, an Air Force Captain in *Armageddon* with Bruce Willis, and finally got a nice close-up shot when I played a Press Reporter in the Tom Hanks' HBO mini-series, *From Earth to the Moon*. All that must have summed up my 15 minutes of fame, because I was never called for anything else after that.

Nineteen ninety-three was a bad year for me in Orlando. I became disillusioned, stopped attending church, and began isolating myself again. I had another DUI and was seriously humbled by having to do Community Service, ironically enough, at Faith Assembly. Becoming so depressed, I found myself popping my prescribed meds of Ativan like candy and swishing it down with wine cooler chasers and cheap beer. Inevitably blacking out and waking up in an ER being forced to drink charcoal. I was "Baker-Acted" twice that year, ending up in a mental ward again, and again. That was the year I was officially labeled "BI-POLAR." Given a new diagnosis to add to the countless others I had already attained to my credit. I wasn't compliant with the many medications and all their countless side effects, so I began just drinking and hanging out in the bars again, using Karaoke as an excuse to further lose myself in alcohol consumption.

I turned out to be pretty good at it, and even won First Prize in a *Sing-Along Talent Contest*, beating one of the Backstreet Boys in his prime, before he was discovered, who I will not name. Okay, I will tell you this much, he was the only Hispanic young talent from Orlando. I was so blessed when they handed me the trophy and a check for $300. I could hardly believe it, felt like I had just won my first Grammy. I know it was nothing, but GOD, who extended some grace and honored me that day, letting me know that He still loved me, even with all my flaws and shortcomings. I also believe that taking the time and dedicating the song to Him, and not being ashamed to do so, was a major factor in my getting the victory that day.

I sang *Unchained Melody by the Righteous Brothers*, and gave the following Intro:

"This is a famous love ballad, that I'm sure you are all familiar with, but tonight I would like to take this opportunity and dedicate it to the One whom without, there would be No Love...

To my Lord and Savior Jesus Christ!"

I couldn't believe how many Christians were in the house. If I were running for President, it would have been a *Landslide!* Yet, while I was getting a small taste of fleeting fame and fortune, I slowly started to notice the widening gap between reality and illusion. I started seeing that I would have to make an ultimate decision between being popular, and pleasing the world, or living for my LORD. My run-ins with famous people and celebrities never left me with the same indelible impression that my spiritual encounters with God did. I began to recognize the great rift that exists between the world and the Kingdom of God.

Upon reading the words in the Bible that proclaimed *friendship with the world as enmity with God,* a profound realization struck me like an abrupt and humbling slap to the face. It was a moment of clarity, a pivotal juncture where I found myself standing at a crossroads, compelled to make a weighty decision, urging me to re-examine the nature of my associations and allegiances. It became clear that I could no longer walk the ambiguous line between the values of the world and the teachings of God. Since that decisive moment, I have never experienced regret for choosing this path. The commitment I made to Jesus has brought immeasurable blessings, guiding my actions, shaping my perspective, and nurturing a profound connection with God. Embracing this unwavering faith, I have discovered a life of true purpose, fulfillment, and spiritual growth. I strongly advise, sincerely hope, and pray that you surrender and come to make the same choice when you come to your crossroads, having to confront the most important decision of your life.

For what will it profit a man if he gains the whole world [wealth, fame, success], but forfeits his soul? Or what will a man give in exchange for his soul? *

{Matthew 16:26/AMP}

Then Jesus went to work on his disciples. "Anyone who intends to come with me must let me lead. You're not in the driver's seat; I am. Don't run from suffering; **embrace it**. Follow me and I'll show you how. Self-help is no help at all. **Self-sacrifice is the way**, my way, to finding yourself, your true self. What kind of deal is it to get everything you want but lose yourself? What could you ever trade your soul for?

{Matthew 16:24-26/MSG}

Choose whom you will serve today!

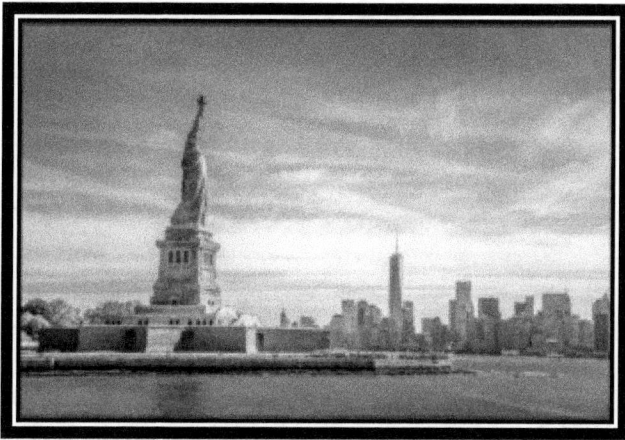

The World, Yourself or God?
{According to Joshua 24:15}

This passage, in essence, seems to be imparting a moral lesson of the importance of self-sacrifice, embracing challenges, and prioritizing one's true self over material or selfish pursuits. It emphasizes that genuine fulfillment comes solely from a selfless approach to life rather than seeking personal gain at any cost, and the dire consequences of our choices.

Chapter Twelve

Divine Intervention

"Lord, we come before your throne of grace in this time of need, thank you for revealing this to your servant by your Holy Spirit... now I ask that you help Nelson come to grips with the reality of what happened to him and allow him to see what he has shucked away in the back of his mind for so long... and bring it into focus so he can admit to what happened, and not continue to blame himself, but forgive himself for what he was a victim to, and be able to surrender it to you. We ask this in agreement, In the name of Jesus."

~ A prayer by Bill Blood

I whispered an amen, and proceeded to ask myself, but was I? After the many doldrums of my Jonah voyage, I finally realized the hit-and-miss approach to spirituality that I had been following was not working for me. I was up one day and down the next; not holding on to the progress I made from time to time. The desire for consistent growth which Jesus had placed in my heart eventually drove me to seek professional Christian counseling. End of '93 I was visiting Calvary Assembly in Winter Park and was referred to a Christian Counselor with the very appropriate name "Bill Blood." He must have been in his late 60s, having much wisdom and discernment.

After coming into his office and nervously rambling on for about 15 minutes, he patiently waited for me to take a breath and pause; Mr. Blood took the opportunity to interject, "You were molested as a child, weren't you?" I was shocked and appalled as someone had just smacked me in the face. "Huh?" I finally muttered. **"You were molested, weren't you?!"** Blood persisted. I would later learn that this revelation was an example of the gift of the Holy Spirit known as a Word of Knowledge, as God revealed to His faithful servant Bill, what had happened to me. I was stunned, and not knowing how to respond to that, I immediately became very uncomfortable.

"Ok," he said, having mercy on me, "We may need to pray about this." Bill Blood took authority and began to pray, as I lowered my head more in embarrassment than reverence. It was a childhood nightmare that I just chose not to recall. As the more Mr. Bill prayed, it started becoming clearer to me the reality, that maybe, just maybe, something had occurred. The cloud somehow lifted, and I began to see it with shocking clarity. Mr. Bill continued persistently to lead me into prayer and coached me that I not only had to forgive myself but also the perpetrator. He strongly advised me to pray out loud and confess that I forgive the person, whether I knew his name or not, and it didn't matter if he was no longer living. I began to repeat the words as Mr. Bill recited the prayer, but when it came to the part of my saying that

I forgave the individual, I got stuck. Clenching my teeth, I became so angry that I just couldn't get myself to say the words. Bill Blood's volume just went up a notch, as he continued praying incessantly and pleading the Blood (of the Lamb) over my mind and soul, as he took authority over every foul spirit, rebuking spirits of unforgiveness, bitterness, hatred, anger, and uncontrollable rage. I felt a surge of rage coming up in me at that point, so much so that I started shaking uncontrollably. After struggling and wrestling with it for what seemed an eternity, I slammed my fists upon my chest, and cried out, "I forgive YOU!" Bill Blood laid gentle hands upon my shoulders, as he kept praying in the Holy Spirit. I sensed the Spirit comforting me as he declared and decreed "Jehovah Shalom" (God's perfect peace) over me. I cried for the remainder of the counseling session; it was like a ton of bricks had been removed from my chest. So light, and saturated with the Spirit of God, I seemed to just float out of his office. So began **the healing process**.

Healing from childhood molestation can be an incredibly challenging and complex process, and forgiveness may or may not happen immediately. It takes time, work and much prayer and reflection, to even find yourself at a juncture where you are ready to forgive, beginning with yourself as well as the abusive party.

NELSON COLÓN

One evening as I got home from work, I grabbed a quick snack and exerted some self-control, choosing not to just plop in front of the tv. I went and sat on my screened-in patio, feeling led to do as Mr. Bill had advised. I began to have a talk with GOD, thanking Him for seeing me through another day, and for my life. Prayed; strayed from asking Him for anything and just started pressing into His presence, praising Him for who He is, and meditating on His goodness. I must have been there close to an hour, just getting intimate with my Creator, as the sun started going down.

At one point I felt so euphoric, I had joined in with the angelic choir. It was so beautiful, sensing such a peace, that tears just began rolling down my face, as I basked in His presence...Till the sun went down, and in the midst of twilight, I began sensing something else. I felt like someone, or something was peering at me, through the bushes of my backyard. It was something intrusive; as I tried to shrug it off, my intense meditation was abruptly interrupted by a high shriek exploding in my eardrums.

Found myself gazing into the glaring beady black eyes of a black cat that had just jumped up seemingly out of nowhere onto my backyard fence. It just stood there glaring right back at me, making a hissing noise. All the hairs on my head seemed to compete with the raised hairs on the body of that cat from hell. I felt fear trying to grip my heart, as I was tempted to throw my slipper at it, but then ...

Something immediately rose up in me, the Spirit of a Warrior. As I heard very distinctly, coming from the black cat, the haunting laughter of a woman mocking me. Hairs stood up even more behind the nape of my neck, as I began to loudly rebuke that Jezebel spirit, "I come against you, not in my name, but in the **Name Above ALL other names!"**

That foul witching spirit just kept mockingly laughing, as the black cat stood fixed without even budging an inch; and so, I continued rebuking with more intensity, increasing my volume and expressing absolute authority,

"The Name to which every knee shall bow, and every tongue has to confess that JESUS Christ is LORD!"

As soon as I named **"JESUS"** that black apparition from hell, just as quickly as it had abruptly appeared, vanished into the shadows. I paced back and forth with newfound freedom and a sense of divine courage like I had just gone one round with the devil, or at least with one of his hellish concubines, **and won!** I sat down on the bare cement floor of my screened-in patio, crossing my legs like Sitting Bull, with continued obstinate focus, meditating and re-entering God's presence while praying in the Spirit.

Experiencing the supernatural once again made evident the call on my life. It not only exposed the evil within my own darkness but also transported me to the brighter spectrum of God's prophetic revelatory knowledge. I went back into the arena of higher learning, challenging my intellect, and studied at City College of Casselberry in Florida. I majored in Private Investigations, a subject that had always intrigued me, graduating Summa Cum Laude, maintaining a 3.9 GPA, and obtaining my Associate of Science degree.

TRANSITION

Began an investigator's apprenticeship program with the Public Defender's Office of Orange County, in Orlando. Still, in its developmental phase, entry-level investigators were hired to g o into the city jails within our jurisdiction, interview the inmates to retrieve their Initial Statements and assist the lawyers in preparing their cases. Amid our daily confusion, I and a team of other Investigators sat side by side in folding chairs and lined-up tables in 'G' Pod at 33rd Street Jail. We were interviewing inmates, while others were climbing the walls impatiently shouting out before their turn, "Hey, when am I gonna see my Public Defender?" There was one inmate that stood out amongst the rest, because, contrary to everyone else, he was calmly waiting his turn on one of the four separate lines that were formed. I noticed him, even more because he just happened to be designated on my line.

Upon his turn, he quietly sat down in front of me, as I proceeded to introduce myself as a representative of the Public Defender's Office, and go through my script of generic questions, "What is your full name, any aliases? So, what happened? Do you have any family members you would need us to contact?" and so on, and so forth. This guy was a cool customer, showing hardly any emotions, unperturbed. Didn't want us to even contact and disturb his father. He claimed he was there because of a simple case of "Mistaken Identity." I recall his first name, Mike. He was black, medium build, and with that short white goatee, he was sporting, resembling a little black Moses. Mike calmly insisted, "I don't want anyone bothering my father, I'll be fine!" When I was done taking his initial statement and all other pertinent information. He signed the paperwork, thanked me, and as he got up to leave, he hesitated as he looked down at the small New Testament Bible that had slipped out from my padfolio. After looking intently at the Bible, then looking at me, he abruptly sat back down. I was a little shaken when he reached out and grabbed my arm, and said, "I'm not through with you yet!" "Excuse me?" I quickly responded, "You know there's no contact,

157

right? Would you like to add something to your statement?" Quickly releasing my arm, Mike just shook his head, and repeated, "No, I'm not through with YOU yet, I am still molding you!" Shocked, I whispered back, "What? You're giving me a word?!" Mike simply nodded, as to say, 'be quiet and listen' and continued giving me what seemed to be a Word from the Lord. At first, with the professional training and orientation I received as an Investigator, I thought this Con may be trying to con me. But immediately, just as soon as that thought entered my head, the Spirit of the LORD convinced me otherwise. I knew it was authentic, when as soon as he nodded, the whole disruptively loud environment in that G-Pod calmed down, and decibels dramatically diminished to a hush. I still heard them, but faintly in the distant background, as I sensed warm oil being poured out upon my head, covering my ears, and seeping deep into my chest. Intently listening I heard the prophet inmate audibly clear as he continued,

"I AM still molding you...
You have not come into this place of your own accord,
I have called you into this place.
I have called you to preach, and you will PREACH,
By My Blood and by the word of your testimony,
I shall set many captives FREE!"

As Mike finished giving me this awe-inspiring word, I almost expected to see wings come out of his back and fly away. The anointing started lifting as the volume and all the ruckus overwhelmingly returned. He got up, and I caught myself reaching out, but simply motioned to him and thanked him. He replied, "That's why I'm here!" as he confidently strolled out from that G-Pod. **"G"** for **GOD!** That's when I knew that God was just setting the stage and granting me the platform to become a Chaplain.

TRANSITION

The road I traveled toward my final spiritual destination was not a sprint; it was much more like a marathon with several ups and downs. As a former Marathon Runner, as well as anyone who has ever run a marathon, will tell you that you go through various stages of inspiration during the run. At some points during the marathon, you will feel a strong sense of euphoria making you think you can keep going forever, whilst at other times you may "hit the wall" feeling so tired and depleted that you just want to stop and quit. This is very similar to what happened to me on my spiritual journey, where I had beautifully inspiring mountaintop experiences. The bliss of heavenly encounters with God, only to still have some low valley contrasting episodes, which would plummet me back into very dark places. Evil dreadful places that would take me into deep states of despair, where I even entertained thoughts of suicide.

One special night, in the realm of dreams, a profound and vivid experience unfolded before me. I found myself immersed in the embrace of an enchanted forest, where an alien cold darkness permeated the air infiltrating my very being with a sense of foreboding and apprehension. Yet, in the depths of my soul, I carried a glimmer of hope. A belief that there was something greater than the surrounding gloom. Instinctively I turned my gaze heavenward and cried out to my heavenly Father. Astonishingly enough, as if in direct response to my plea, the path before me parted and widened, revealing a hazy dimmer of light which seemed to dance through the clearing of the trees.

A surge of warmth enveloped my spirit as the sunlight tenderly caressed my face, and as if carried on a metaphysical breeze, the ethereal melodies of celestial music resonated deep within my soul. It was a symphony of angelic choruses beckoning me towards a great gathering that awaited just beyond the crest of the hill. In that moment of awakening, I was imbued with an indescribable certainty; a glimpse into the transcendent realm of heaven itself. Through this dream, God revealed that even in the darkest of times, when we feel utterly lost and alone, our heartfelt pleas of desperation are heard on high. As I emerged from the depths of slumber, the prophetic dream's imprint remained etched upon my consciousness. Carrying with me the indelible revelatory knowledge that God, in His infinite wisdom, granted me a glimpse into the eternal. An assurance that there is a realm beyond this earthly existence, where the light of love forever shines, and where we shall ultimately be reunited with our loved ones. This dream served as a sacred reminder, a testament to the eternal nature of our souls and the divine destiny that awaits us, solely in the condition, of our acceptance of the Christ. For no one ever shed their sinless blood for us but the Lamb.

I once heard a pastor preach that people are much more like Ocean Liners than they are like swimming ducks. We want to turn quickly and swiftly on our life's journey, especially after powerful revelations and anointed encounters with God. We imagine that we have now dramatically changed the course of our lives, the same way a duck quickly changes direction on the water's surface. But in truth, we are much more like Ocean Liners that take a long time to change course. We must set our sights on the end goal and settle in for a long marathon run before we can pick the fruits of a slow change in the right direction, which ultimately takes us to the place where ...

TRANSITION

God has laid out a wonderful destiny for us.

Chapter Thirteen

Deliverance
Likened to St. Paul I could relate to having a thorn in my flesh.
{2 Corinthians 12:7}
God allowed a messenger of satan, a dark entity which delivered that
nightmarish rude awakening, catapulting me to search for the LORD's
divine infinite wisdom. God assigned this appointed time to prepare
me, not only to be inducted into the Navy's Basic Training, but His
Divine Boot Camp, where I attained a deeper spiritual epiphany of
who HE was, who He still is, and who He forever shall be,
the Great I AM!

NELSON COLÓN

Flash back from *July of 1995* *

*I experienced a supernatural breakthrough which was a very significant spiritual milestone in my life, finally leading to my **deliverance**.*

Although it wasn't until the Summer when I got word from my half-sister Gloria that our father was fighting Alzheimer's. Gloria was a husky rambunctious female version of our father, resembling him to a tee except for the long black hair, not just in facial appearance, but had the same volatile anger issue. I heard through the grapevine that she had taken on a couple of police officers in an all-out fist fight in the town of Ponce.

I immediately flew out to Puerto Rico and spent quality time with my dying father. Although I know most of my family felt vindicated thinking, he was just reaping what he had sown all his life. Despite this, I went and just expressed my love for my father, and by doing so I believe I was fulfilling the fifth commandment. "To honor your father and mother", not just honor your father only if he deserves it, but to equally honor them both. I find comfort and peace in knowing I did that regardless. As I approached him, he would try to get up as if he initially recognized me and was attempting to greet me but would just as quickly slump back down onto the couch and drift off again looking away from me to the wall. I would sit down by his side and put on some old westerns. My father loved westerns, especially ones that starred his favorite cowboy, John "the Duke" Wayne. I would try to get his attention, *"¡Mira Papi, Una Película de Vaquero!"*[44] hoping he would express some excitement and recall when I used to call out to him as a child in Puerto Rico, with crossed legs sitting too close to the tube. Praying that he would not only recognize his favorite show, but his son. He would try to look towards the TV to see what I was talking about, and just as quickly fade back to staring aimlessly at the opposite wall in the living room. I still sat with him, put my arms around him, and hugged him as tight as my grip would allow. I spent endless days with him that way, just loving him, trying to engage him by talking about things in the past.

164

TRANSITION

I recalled the time when I was nine, and he took me to see the NY Yankees play a doubleheader against the Detroit Tigers to win both games. I loved those "Bronx Bombers" ever since. I told him that Jesus loved him regardless of all the terrible sins that he had committed in his past and was willing to forgive him. I quietly prayed every day over him till the day I had to leave and fly back to Orlando. Although my father was infamous for using and abusing women, God in His tender mercies still showed him favor, by blessing him with Norma. A God-fearing, soft-spoken, gentle native woman of Puerto Rico. She had shared with me briefly, that she had her pastor come to the house and pray over him with some fellow believers, and that the pastor felt in his heart that my father had repented. She claims when the pastor was praying, he looked deep into my father's eyes and witnessed tears welling up. So, who knows, only GOD truly knows the heart of a man. I would hope, for his sake as well as for the sake of Christ's name, that he was truly remorseful and repentant.

In the Living Word, *Psalm 130:3,4* establishes this truth:
For if the LORD should mark iniquity against us, who could stand? **But thanks be to GOD, for there is forgiveness through Jesus Christ** *that we may be saved and learn to revere Him.*
There is still **power in the Blood of Jesus Christ** to cleanse us from all sin and unrighteousness.[45] Although, it is up to us to **repent, and accept what Jesus has already done for us at Calvary's Cross.**

I took one last picture with my father before I left him, after having spent that last week with him, knowing in my heart that I would not see him alive again. I kissed him, hugged him one last time, and whispered to him,

"El Señor te Amas y No Vino para condenarte, pero para perdonarte. Yo también te amo y te perdono, Papi." [46]

That was in the summer of '95.
Two months later, I flew back to Ponce.
To bury my father.

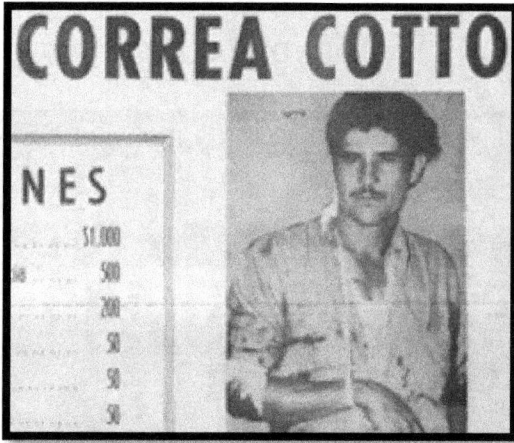

September 25, 1995

As I looked at my father's plastic-coated memorial card with the Lord's prayer, **"Secundino Cotto Colón"** stared out at me. My father's last name was Cotto, but in Hispanic culture, both paternal and maternal names are printed on all legal documents. I was supposed to be a "Cotto", I thought, as I recall my mother's explanation of how I ended up with "Colón" instead ...

When I was born in NYC, my father filled out the birth certificate information with his full name, as he was accustomed to doing in Puerto Rico. Gouverneur Hospital documented my name on the official New York Birth Certificate assuming the last (maternal) surname of his mother's maiden name was my paternal surname. When my mother made my father aware of the error, he never tried to change it. He thought it was best to just leave it alone, for the "Cotto family" name was infamous in Ponce. A distant cousin from my father's side was a wanted killer and the first legendary outlaw from Puerto Rico. The infamous **Correa Cotto**. * The Cottos even garnered enough infamy to have a street in Ponce referenced by their family name, **"La Calle de Los Cotto's."** [47]

*[**DEAD or ALIVE**]

At my father's burial, as I bent down to pick up a handful of dirt to throw into my father's grave, unknowingly picked up a rock as well. As I threw the dirt onto the metal casket, the embedded rock rang forth like the Liberty Bell. The haunting sound startled everybody throughout the entire cemetery, including me, as I **felt something lift off me.** I sensed deliverance as I cried out,

"Yo te perdono Papi ...
I forgive you!"

Years of subtle resentment towards my father for having allowed me to grow up with the insecurity of rejection and lack of identity were gone. As well as feelings of unworthiness and self-loathing were somehow miraculously and instantaneously lifted off my mind, and injured emotions. The Power of Forgiveness.

TRANSITION

Delving deeper into my soul and uprooting a world of unresolved hurt and anger. I was being healed internally in my spirit-man, delivered from all passive-aggressiveness, and uncontrollable outbursts of rage.

I felt such a peaceful, intense sense of elation after I boarded the plane and left Puerto Rico. I came back to the States feeling complete and whole, emotions intact, something I don't ever recall growing up.

Although I never got any condolences from anyone in my family for having lost my father, I had such a surpassing peace not to hold it against them. I chose to understand. I was the one who really needed to release the pain and unforgiveness in order for my inner-hurting child to begin to heal and mature. I closed the door to my father's cursed legacy and was able to finally bury, along with him, all the pain which ensued.

Fast Forwarding ...

To exactly the **10th year anniversary** of my father's death and burial:
September 25th, 2005
"In GOD's Appointed Time"
the LORD blessed me with yet another son ...

NELSON COLÓN

~Seth Nelson Colón~

Born from the womb of my present beautiful wife
Maritza Santiago (De-Colón),
My promised helpmate. Another native New Yorican, like myself, is
also from the LES area of Manhattan, where I was born. Her parents,
just like my parents, happened to also be natives from Ponce, Puerto
Rico. Not a coincidence. She was my princess, just waiting for her
prince, brought up in the Baruch Projects on FDR Drive.
Seth, my youngest son is a testament to the fact as the second living
witness, in addition to his older brother Nathaniel, that the cursed
'Cotto' legacy of their earthly grandfather was indeed **broken**.
Beginning **a blessed legacy** and spiritual generation **by** our Heavenly
Father, adopting us as His children born by the Spirit, via the spiritual
Bloodline of His Only Begotten,
Jesus the Christ (Yeshua the Messiah).

TRANSITION

After marrying Maritza Santiago

in 2003, I relocated back to NYC.

NELSON COLÓN

My LORD saw fit to grant me favor and promote me once again, this time as a doorman for the professors of NYU.

FASTER THAN A SPEEDING BULLET...

The staff and professors kept asking how I managed to walk in off the street, without being a member of Local 32 BJ, and still get considered for such a prestigious position. "Who do you know?" they'd ask curiously. My answer was always the same: "Jesus, of course! Who else would I need to know?"

TRANSITION

**In conclusion, toward the end of 1995,
I entered 1996 a changed man.**

To be **"totally delivered"** from drugs, alcohol, and all forms of self-inflicted abuse means that you have achieved complete freedom from the hold that these substances and behaviors once had on you. It means that you are no longer controlled by the desire to use or engage in harmful activities, and that you have overcome the physical and psychological dependence that can accompany addiction.

The fallacy "Once a Junkie, always a Junkie" suggests that addiction is a lifelong struggle that cannot be overcome, but my experience proved otherwise. God has shown that with determination, faith, and support, it is possible to break free from the cycle of addiction and live a healthy, fulfilling life.

Walking in the power of His Spirit means that you are relying on the higher power to guide and strengthen you in your journey towards recovery. This can provide a sense of purpose, hope and support that is essential for long-term success.

My ongoing record of 25-plus years remaining clean and sober is a testament to the power of this approach. My experience of being miraculously healed of Hepatitis-C is another example of the power of faith and the potential of transformation. This healing serves as a reminder that with applied faith, **all things are indeed possible**, and that even in the face of adversity, we can find hope and strength in the Word.

In Summation,
my story is a powerful testimonial to the fact that addiction can be overcome, and that there is hope for those struggling
with this same issue.
By relying on faith, support, personal strength,
and trust in the Almighty.
Anyone can achieve the same remarkable levels of freedom and healing.
May my example serve as an inspiration to others who may need to be on a similar journey...
from Victory to ongoing Victory.

"For whom the Son sets free is Free Indeed!"
{John 8:36}

"It's a new day.
Yesterday's failures are redeemed at sunrise."
— **Todd Stocker, Dancing with God**

Summation

"Run the Good Race!"

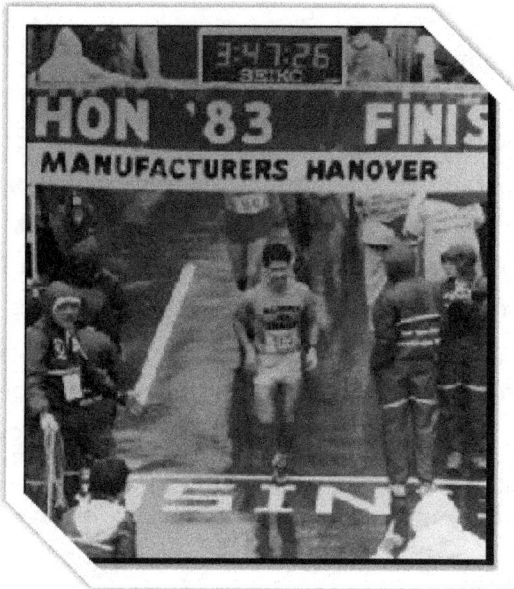

*{In this **photo FINISH**, you can see me stepping on **SIN**.*
I believe it's God's way of confirming to me that
***HE** has literally given me the victory over sin.}*

<u>*January 1998*</u>

I ran two NYC marathons back in 1982 and '83 in Jesus' name. I also ran the 1989 Citrus Bowl Half Marathon when I initially relocated to Orlando, Florida. I ran the Disney Marathon in 1998, my final marathon before reaching the age of 40. I was able to finish the entire 26.2 miles, solely by the grace of God. My time paled in comparison to the marathons of my early twenties. It still gave me a sense of elation and accomplishment when I crossed that finish line one last time at Disney World.

In my continued pursuit of fitness, I joined the Fitness Centre at Florida Hospital's launching of Celebration Health in the town of Celebration that same year. As an incentive to remain fit going into my forties, I also became certified as a fitness trainer and began conducting cardio-kickboxing classes at Celebration Health. If we're faithful in little, God shows Himself faithful in so much more, for I began getting job offers from many other fitness facilities throughout Orlando. That was around the same time Billy Blanks had just introduced his infomercials of "Tai-Bo", and so I quickly became known as the Billy Blanks of Central Florida, as my new position of Kickboxing Instructor became in high demand.

Around that same time, I also became involved with Chuck Colson's Prison Fellowship events throughout Florida. Also volunteered at Cherokee County Jail's Chaplain Department in Holly Springs, GA.

Tending God's temple, taking care of the body, as well as keeping the spirit-man alive and well within me, by allowing His Spirit to renew the spirit of my mind daily by studying (Torah) scripture and abiding in His Holy Presence; staying active and plugged into the ministry whereas He has called me.

To Fulfill the work of an Evangelist.
A Certified Chaplain in GOD's Special Forces.

TRANSITION

An Active Member of the Body of Christ: To be a Chaplain in God's Special Forces and an active member of the Body of Christ means that you are a spiritual leader who serves in a ministry dedicated to supporting and guiding members of the armed forces, law enforcement, and other emergency service personnel. As a Chaplain, you provide counseling, mentorship, and pastoral care to individuals and families in times of crisis, grief, or spiritual need. You also offer religious services, perform sacraments, and facilitate spiritual retreats for those in your care. Being an active member of the Body of Christ means that you are part of a community of believers who follow Jesus Christ as their Lord and Savior. You share a common faith and commitment to God's teachings and strive to live your life in accordance with His will. As an active member, you participate in worship services, Bible studies, prayer groups, and other activities that help you deepen your relationship with God and build relationships with fellow believers. You also serve others through acts of compassion, outreach, and evangelism, seeking to share the love of Christ with those around you.

Overall, being a Chaplain in God's Special Forces and an active member of the Body of Christ involves serving others, sharing God's love, and living out your faith in both **word and deed**. An Active Member of **J.E.S.U.S.**

J >ehovah's E >lite S >pecial U >nit S >quad

Hail to my Commander in Chief, my LORD and King Adonai. The Mighty Lion of Judah, Yeshua the Messiah. He remains faithful to complete the noble work He already has commenced. As the Author and Finisher of our Faith, we place our trust not just in ourselves, but in Him, the Savior of our souls. Therefore, this marks just the commencement of our journey, not the conclusion. Not...

The End.

Epilogue

Influenced by the wisdom and teachings of Jim Cymbala, David Wilkerson, and Nicky Cruz, Nelson's memoir invites readers to ponder the profound questions that echo within their own souls. The purpose in pain, the quest for love amidst loneliness, and the unfathomable depths of hope in seemingly hopeless situations, become threads interwoven with Nelson's story, prompting deep introspection and contemplation.

May Nelson's story serve as beacon of light to all who dare confront their own demons, question societal labels and stigmas, and embrace the courage to embark on their own journeys toward healing and deliverance.

Let this memoir stand as a testament to the phenomenal power of the human spirit, especially when it's aligned with the Spirit of the great Divine, His purposes and plan for one's life. A power combined that can overcome the darkest of circumstances and enlighten the path towards a brighter, more hopeful future.

As the curtains close on this extraordinary tale, one thing remains certain: Nelson Colón's legacy will endure, inspiring generations to come, and reminding us that the pursuit of hope knows no boundaries.

About the Author:

Nelson Colón,
a Native New Yorker,
born in the Lower East Side of Manhattan,
and raised in Brooklyn.
Former Navy Airman,
an autonomous Chaplain serving churches and communities in the
Atlanta-Metro area of Northern Georgia (Acworth, Kennesaw, KSU).
Resides there presently with his wife and son.
Any questions pertaining to any issues
that may have been addressed in this book,
please feel free to email the Chaplain directly:
ChaplainNC@Gmail.com
Thank you.

"A Song of Love"
My heart is overflowing with a good theme.
I recite my composition concerning the King.
My tongue is the pen of a ready writer.
{Psalm / Chapter 45: Verse 1/NKJV}

Reflections

"From: James, a servant of God and of the Lord Jesus Christ. To: Jewish Christians scattered everywhere. Greetings!

Dear brothers, is your life full of difficulties and temptations? Then be happy, for when the way is rough, your patience has a chance to grow. So let it grow, and don't try to squirm out of your problems. When your patience is finally in full bloom, then you will be ready for anything, strong in character, full and complete. If you want to know what God wants you to do, ask him, and he will gladly tell you, for he is always ready to give a bountiful supply of wisdom to all who ask him; he will not resent it. But when you ask him, be sure that you really expect him to tell you, for a doubtful mind will be as unsettled as a wave of the sea that is driven and tossed by the wind."

James 1:1-6 (TLB)

And we know that all that happens to us is working
for our good if we love God
and fit into His plans.
Romans 8:28 (TLB)

Like Orson Welles' character's sled, 'Rosebud' my trikes symbolized my innocence before becoming stained with sin. When I had my two trikes, I also had my siblings and both parents with me. Our family was complete. I was a child, without any preoccupation or knowledge of the ugly scope of reality.

What I will say is that I descended into that musty old dungeon, a relatively happy, innocent young trusting boy, but ascended as someone very different. Perhaps no one noticed the immediate change in me, but I was never the same again afterward. Not even the thought of my Rosebud, my beloved tricycle could make me smile again with the same hope and simple faith that had been mine before.

I wandered aimlessly afterward, only this time there was no emergency medical procedure that could fix what had happened. The mere passage of time also did nothing to make the pain and shock go away. I grew fearful of the world and didn't know how to trust anyone from that point on. Growing angry as I shut down my emotions.

These behavioral patterns were a foreshadowing of my later abuse of alcohol and my eventual attempts at self-medication by numbing my brain with cocaine and harder narcotics like heroin. I became introverted.

Later during my adolescence, as I underwent puberty, all these abuses contributed detrimentally to my ultimately confused sexual identity, inevitably driving me to the point where I lost myself in a dark world of lasciviousness. For more than thirty years I locked away the awful truth in the deepest recesses of my mind...those memories of the underground dungeon and the unspeakable violation the strangely perverted predator exposed me to. These seeds of evil eventually grew to maturity and produced a bitter harvest in my life.

TRANSITION

Looking back with 20/20 hindsight it's easy to see where I could have played it differently to avoid most of the sorrow I experienced. Even though I could not have prevented my father from throwing my mother down a flight of stairs and couldn't have foreseen that jumping on a bed would have caused me such serious bodily harm. I could have obeyed my mother and refused to get on the bike with that boy and even after experiencing the perverse evil which I fell prey to in that dark basement, I could have thrown myself at the feet of the Cross much sooner than I did. It is my sincere prayer that my story will prompt anyone with similar scenarios to reach out to those loving Hands which still bear the scars of the nails which pierced the Prince of Peace so that we might have a new life, and experience His transitional transformation, saving grace, and deliverance.

God always has a far greater plan for our lives than the one we have for ourselves; He is truly able to do exceedingly, abundantly more than anything we can ever imagine. I started sensing the prompting of the Holy Spirit to write down my experiences and journal the spiritual progress I experienced on my journey as I drew closer to the Light. At that time, I thought this might be a helpful tool to keep track of my progress and review some of the revelations which God gave me as I continued to walk in obedience. But as I reflect upon my life and look back now, journaling not only turned out to be a useful therapeutic tool for self-analysis and spiritual inventory but eventually became the rough draft for the chapters of this book. My history, sanctified by GOD became "HIS-Story" for HIS Glory turning it all around for good! The Bible teaches us that we will eventually overcome the evil continually plaguing our lives if we don't lose heart, and get aligned with the Great Divine, and His Kingdom purposes.

By the Blood of the Lamb and by the word of our Testimony... we overcame the evil one.
{Revelation 12:11}

This book is the *Word of my Testimony*, and I am confident that it conveys the unmistakable ring of truth which we all instinctively recognize when someone shares an accurate account of their experiences. While perusing through the various chapters of my life, I sincerely hope that most of my readers will never have to encounter the insanity, and utter hopelessness that comes with addiction to drugs and alcohol. However, I understand that each person faces their own personal challenges that might lead them to a place of despair. If you find yourself in such a situation, I hope and pray that my story can be a source of inspiration for you.

Even though I may have descended into the depths of hell itself, I was never beyond the saving hands of Jesus Christ, as He reached down with *an outstretched arm,* and pulled me out of that terrible pit. Therefore, I am convinced that no one on God's good earth is ever truly beyond salvation. I would ask you to remember that people look at the outward appearance and make their judgment accordingly, whilst God looks at the heart of a man. Although people might at first glance see me as a man who's just been jaded, I can see how God was always present during all my folly and my chaotic unstable life. He was just **molding me**; allowing me to experience these traumatic events to qualify me, to become a vessel of compassion for those who might presently be experiencing similar circumstances in their lives. Take heart in knowing that our Heavenly Father is the God of All Comfort[1]:

"Praise be to the God and Father of our Lord Jesus Christ, the Father of compassion and the God of all comfort, who comforts us in all our troubles so that we,
in turn, can comfort those in any trouble with the same comfort we ourselves have received from God."
{2 Corinthians 1:3,4}

---

1.   http://biblehub.com/bsb/2_corinthians/1.htm

If you find, as you reflect upon your own life, that you can relate to just one traumatic event, please allow yourself to be open to the possibility that there is a GOD who wants to take that negative experience and turn it all around for your good. If He was able to do it for me, He would be more than able to do it for **you**.

Take a moment now and answer these questions honestly:

_Were you ever molested or abused as a child?

_Did you grow up without the security of a father present?

_Did you grow up in a tough neighborhood, bullied in school, and joined a club or gang to fit in or feel accepted, protected, and no longer victimized?

_Did you grow up with a low self-image and self-loathing?

_Have you ever turned to drugs and/or alcohol to numb your feelings of inadequacy and unresolved issues of rejection or other emotional pain?

_Did you ever feel confused or struggled with your own sexual identity, causing you to succumb to a lascivious lifestyle?

_Have you ever delved into the occult out of curiosity or to try and gain control over your situations?

_Have you ever had thoughts of wanting to harm yourself or end your life?

_Were you ever diagnosed, labeled, and/or stigmatized with a mental condition or disability?

If you answered 'yes' to any of these questions and you experience mental challenges or other issues of spiritual oppression which are like my personal experiences which I have described in this book, don't despair. You are a good candidate for the wonderful Healing Hands of Jesus Christ.

Seek the LORD for Wisdom, Guidance, and Comfort.
Speak with a Professional Therapist, Certified Counselor, and/or Clergy. Ideally who's been "**Born-Again**" according to *John 3:3*

And if you have been fortunate enough to escape any of these post-traumatic events in your life, please remember that Jesus is the only One who can ultimately grant you safe passage into Eternal Life when this temporal life is over.

I would encourage you, right now, to pray this model prayer or even better, **say what comes from your heart**, and ask Jesus to come into your own personal life and guide you to the spiritual place of destiny which He has preordained for you:

*"Jesus, I not only acknowledge you as my Savior, **but accept You as the LORD of my life! You are the Only Begotten Son and Express Image of Almighty GOD**; reconciling us back to Our Heavenly Father when You died for our sins on the Cross at Calvary. I ask you to forgive me for my disbelief and **accept you as my personal Lord and Savior**. I humbly ask you to wash away all of my sins and unrighteousness; write my name in your Book of Life, lead me on your divine path and place upon me Your holy robe of righteousness, so You and I will be together forever. In Your Holy Name, **the Name whereby we must all be saved, the Name of Yeshua (Jesus) the Messiah, Amen.**"*

*If you declare with your mouth, **"Jesus is Lord"**, and **believe in your heart that God raised him from the dead, you will be saved**. For it is with your heart that you believe and are justified, and it is with your mouth that you profess your faith and are saved. {Romans 10:9,10}*

Now allow God's Spirit to take you on a journey and adventure of self-discovery. You will be amazed at what delightful surprises He has in store for you. As I have taken you through the reflections of my own life, relating to you the spiritual *transition* thereof, and memoirs of my **Madness to the Miraculous.**

TRANSITION

You should have gathered by now that I have experienced many of the events covered by the list of questions I have asked of you, and yet I am still here to tell the tale. Which proves that the power of God is greater than any evil you could ever fall prey to in this life. As much as I may have felt lost and hopeless as I went through each lonely chapter of my life, I always found that **"Jehovah Shammah"** (The LORD GOD who is always there) will show up and prove that His grace was, and always will be, greater than ALL our sin.

He intervened in every aspect of my life, no matter how bad I perceived it to be, and showed Himself **Strong** on my behalf, even when I was at my weakest point. My life is a living testimony of the following scripture:

But He said to me,
"My grace is sufficient for you, for my power is made perfect in your weakness."
Therefore, I will boast all the more gladly about my weaknesses, so that Christ's power may rest upon me.
That is why, for Christ's sake, I delight in weaknesses, insults, hardships, persecutions, and in difficulties.
For when I am weak, then I am strong. *~ St. Paul*
{2 Corinthians 12:9-10}

As I have already stated, if you have been fortunate enough **not** to have gone through such dramatic episodes in your life as I have, count your blessings, although you still need to **Repent** and look to Jesus to keep you safe from all the evils of this fallen world. We can't afford to gamble with our souls, thinking we're all right, yet be spiritually blinded by our own self-righteousness.

I thank God that, even though I had to undergo these trials and tribulations in my own personal life, through it all I came to know and experience the Living God in the person of Jesus Christ. I can say, with all truth and sincerity, that I know beyond a shadow of a doubt that there is a God and that by His grace, and His saving grace alone, I have been truly blessed and highly favored. I count all my tribulations as gain and I thank God that I have been given this opportunity to share them with you, knowing that my experiences will ultimately be a blessing if only you will declare yourself willing to learn from them.

It is my prayer for you, as well as for those who have their own supernatural tales to tell, that through the reading of this testimonial, you may be imparted with a touch from on High. Just as His Spirit broke every generational curse off me, may He also set you free from every yoke of disbelief, that may still be keeping you from accepting the only truth that can and will indeed set you free!

So, I leave you with this and conclude:

I pray that the spiritual scales may come off your eyes
and that you might have your own **"Born Again"** Mountain-Top
experience and encounter Him,
the only One who can save you.
For Jesus himself said, in John 3:3:
"Most definitely I say to you,
(place your own name right here)
*Unless you have been **born from above**, you will not be able to see the*
Kingdom of God!"

Jesus Himself, who came not to condemn but to save. The One who shed His sinless, precious Blood for you and me, and for all who would accept this gift of Life, the only One worthy to sit at the Right Hand of the Power of Almighty GOD, making Him the Ultimate High(est) Priest. Jesus didn't say you had to be of any religion, race, creed, or color, neither Jew, nor Gentile, nor Catholic, nor Protestant, nor Greek, nor Muslim, nor Buddhist. Or a part of any other conjured up man's dogma or doctrine. Religion is man-made. Created to bring political control, and confusion not unity. But GOD is not an author of confusion. **Religion** not only creates **confusion,** but also breeds division.

Jesus said ALL you must be is **Born from Above.** Accept and Receive Him as **the Way, the Truth, and the Life,** and your name shall be written in the **Lamb's Book of Life**.

I urge you to give heed to that heavenly power you sense right now, drawing you closer to a personal encounter with the Living Christ. He stands at the door of your heart and knocks, waiting for you to **open**. Jesus is not interested in your religion, political affiliation, sexual preference, or lifestyle, but only in **you** as a person and He is waiting patiently for you to invite Him in, so that He may come inside and have a feast of **Abundant Life** with you.

https://takingtherainbowback.com

<u>Questions to Ponder with Biblical Underpinning</u>:
_What was the most terrible thing that ever happened to you?
Genesis 37:1-11
_How did it change you?
Job 1
_Can you now see GOD's Hand in it?
Jeremiah 29:11
Romans 8:38-39
_Are you willing to allow GOD to transition and transform you into a vessel of compassion
to be able to bring GOD's comfort to others?
2 Corinthians 1:3,4
_Are you willing to admit your weaknesses, so Christ can make you strong?
2 Corinthians 12:9-10
_Wouldn't you like to be Born from above and baptized by His Spirit?
John 3:3

TRANSITION

AMAN!

A Poem by Nelson Colón*

There once was a man, born King of Kings,

Yet He wore no crown, nor bore any rings.

He spoke to us in parables, you see,

To reveal what was hidden, to set the truth free.

In a world shrouded in utter darkness,

He brought God's light, so wondrous and starkness.

For the truth, He was cruelly persecuted,

In pure innocence, He was executed.

But instead of leaving us with condemnation,

He gave us the blessed hope of salvation.

Oh, what love it must have taken,

For God to remain unshaken,

To fulfill the great mission

That only His begotten Son could do,

Bringing His Father's message of undying love,

To this dying world, to me and to you.

Placed upon that cursed tree,

For all mankind to see,

He who was without sin,

Became sin for you and me.

Many still say He was just a man.

A man!? Just a man?

I believe He was far more than that,

And for Him, I'll take my stand.

Not I alone, but many believe,

Willing to lay down their lives ...

Declaring Jesus was, is, and forever shall be,

The miracle-working God in the flesh, the Almighty, the One and only Divine.

Through His sacrifice, we are freed from sin and death,

By His resurrection, we claim victory with every breath.

NELSON COLÓN

To conquer the works of the enemy,

And become all He meant us to be.

When all tribulations have passed,

And this world as we know it is done,

Our lives in Christ will have just begun.

So, let's keep singing praises to His Name,

Offering prayers, steadfast and the same.

Let our hearts remain firm and never waver, So,

Jesus Christ can truly be our personal Lord and Savior!

* Copyrighted by Chaplain NC

Publisher & Creator of New Creation Concepts

Acknowledgments

Children are a gift from the Lord. They are a reward from Him. Like ARROWS in the hand of the ARCHER. How joyful is the man whose quiver is full of them. —Psalm 127

Nethaniel, Nehemiah, and Seth

La Familia Colón

Sethy

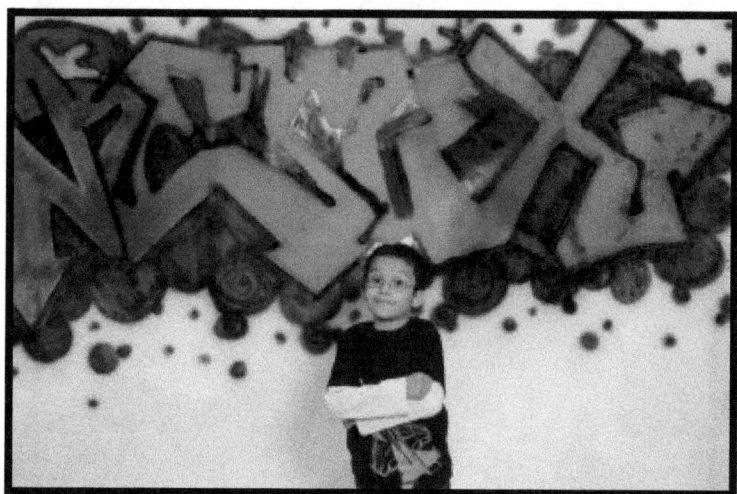

"Our Blessed Boy"
Seth has always been in Advanced Honor classes.
Not only academically gifted but has an ear for Music.
Plays the trumpet in his High School Band.
He also has a great eye for photography, a gifted artist.
Gifted also in writing and helped me Co-edit this book.
Your mother and I are extremely proud of you son,
and we love you very much.
God bless you!

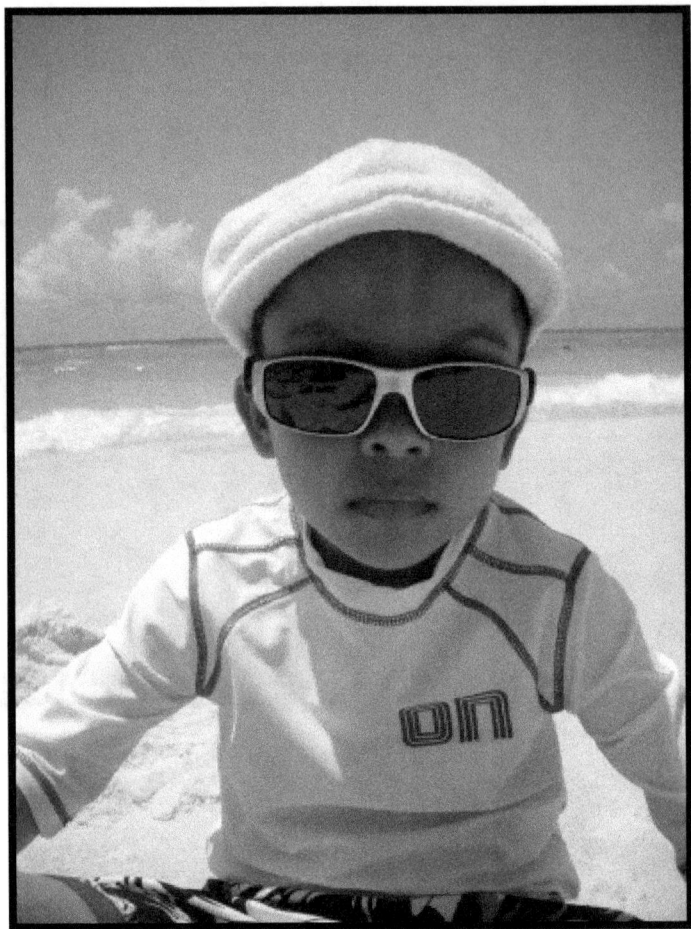

Seth on Destin Beach

TRANSITION

Nethaniel and Family

NELSON COLÓN

My Firstborn Nethaniel

TRANSITION

Nethaniel and Nehemiah

NELSON COLÓN

Nethaniel with Grandma

TRANSITION

Nehemiah

Jesus reaching Out to You
with an Outstretched Arm!

TRANSITION

"Abuelita"

AltaGracia Cruz

NELSON COLÓN

"Mami"

Dora Hilda Rodríguez

IN LOVING MEMORY OF

of the fabulous

Gladys Rodriguez Cruz

July 21, 1933 — December 17, 2023

Please join us at her wake
Saturday 23rd December,
4pm to 8pm.

Ortiz Funeral Home
201 Havemeyer St,
Brooklyn, NY 11211

The Rodriguez Clan

TRANSITION

School of Hard Knocks

Roy Jones Jr.

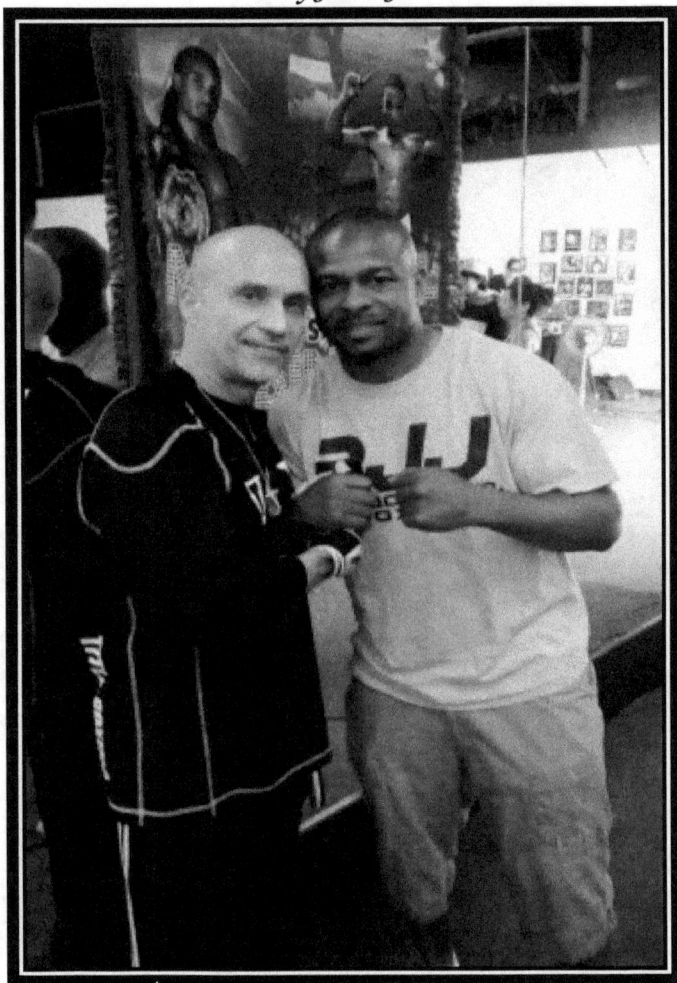

TRANSITION

Evander "Real Deal" Holyfield

NELSON COLÓN

Erik Estrada

TRANSITION

Maritza Santiago-Colón

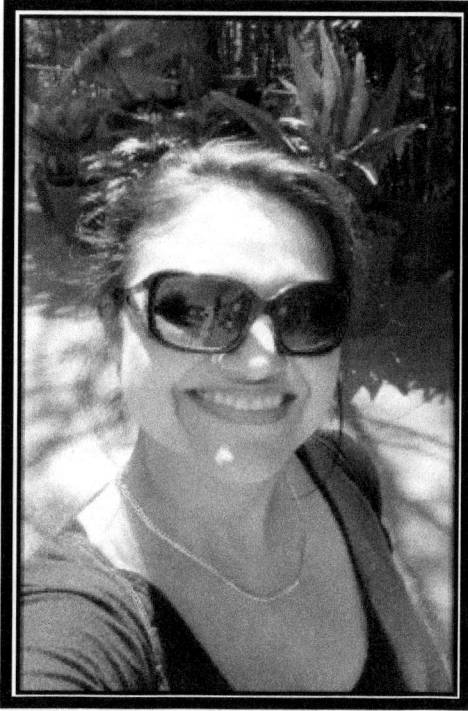

Kingdom Minds Advancing
Campus Crusades for Christ
The King's College

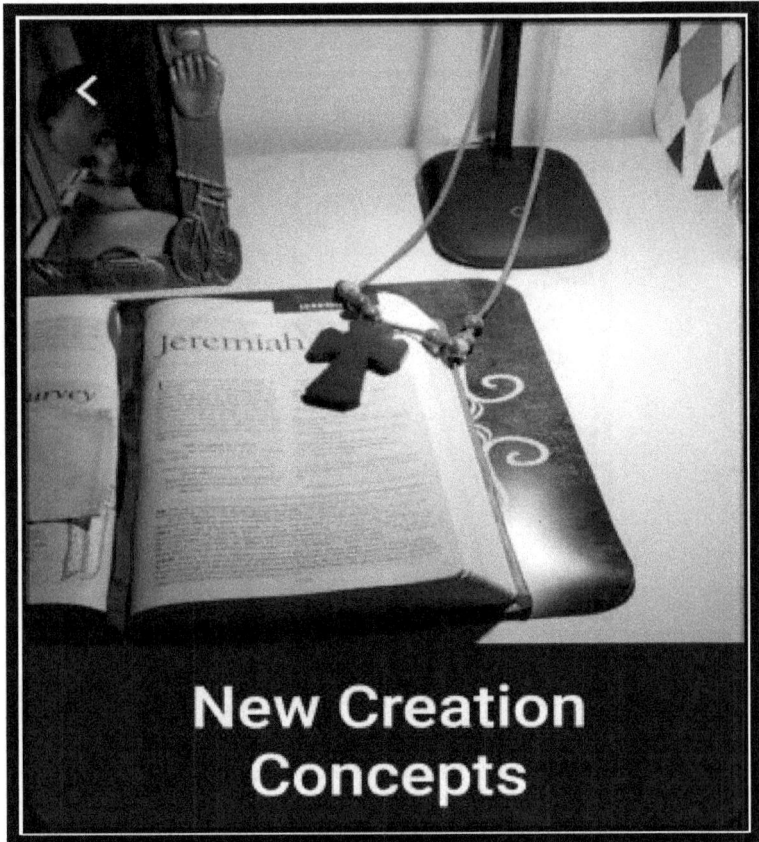

New Creation
Concepts

Behold,
I say unto you a new thing I will do, says the Lord.
{2 Corinthians 5:17}

The Vision

As we enter a new season, although still faced with insurmountable odds, there are still endless opportunities for us to pull ahead and succeed.

We shouldn't go by our feelings, which can be very misleading during these times of financial struggles. We need to follow the Word of GOD and "Live by Faith!" which is *the substance of things hoped for, and the evidence of things not seen."*

{Hebrews 11:1}

As Believers, faith is the only thing we know that pleases GOD. More reason for us to pull together as one body, corporately praying, and working together towards rising above our financial difficulties, looking beyond our denominational preferences and ethnic prejudices.

We can all volunteer to help each other with our ministries, by also cooperatively and practically assisting each other with our resources. After all, isn't that how the former Church did it?

We can work a whole lot more efficiently toward fulfilling what GOD has given for us to do, if we are no longer bogged down by debt, and are financially free to serve GOD and His Kingdom's purposes. We wouldn't have to depend on secular bank owners for loans *"neither a lender nor a borrower be"* if we would help support one another within the Body of Christ.

Let's learn to trust our Heavenly Father above all else. But let's also learn to trust and share our financial resources with each other, so we can rise above our debt and break free from the financial bondage of this Babylonian banking system.

Together, the Body of Christ can soar like an eagle, far above the tempest and the storm, even in this season of trial and recession.

The Body of Christ should not be hurting or divided. We shouldn't be competing; instead, we should be genuinely helping one another to reach a state of equality. This way, the Body can achieve complete equilibrium and heal.

{2 Corinthians 8:13-15}

That should be the way of the Latter Church, which was mandated by our Lord Jesus Christ. Anything less is not truly representing the Kingdom of GOD. We need to remain steadfast in encouraging one another toward attaining the hope, the future, and abundant life in Christ that He promised us as His Church, His Chosen, and His Beloved Bride.

Creating and publishing New Creation Concepts is my act of faith, believing and trusting first and foremost in our Heavenly Father. Praying that He would place it in our hearts to stand and work together as One Body in Christ Jesus.

"For I know the plans I have for you," declares the LORD,
"Plans to prosper you and not harm you,
plans to give you hope and a future!"
{Jeremiah 29:11}

The Mission

I am an Ordained Minister via the National Association of Christian Ministers (NACM); I am also an Autonomous Chaplain, independently certified through The International Federation of Christian Chaplains (IFCC). Doing the work of an Evangelist:
"But you be watchful in all things, endure afflictions, do the work of an evangelist, and fulfill your ministry."
{2 Timothy 4:5/NKJV}
Being the Church and bringing the Church to people who can't make it to church. Going into the streets (La Iglesia de la Calle), the highways, and byways:
"Go to the highways, and back alleys urging people to come in, that my house may be filled!"
{Luke 14:23/CEB}
Going into the hospitals, the jails, crossing the line which divides Church from State, and going even into the schools, taking back our children, compelling them to look toward the Kingdom of Heaven, and to our Lord and King,
Jesus as the answer to all their questions.
Thus, fulfilling the Great Commission:

And Jesus came and spoke to them saying,
"All Authority has been given to me in heaven and on earth...Go
therefore and make disciples of all the nations, baptizing them in the
name of the Father, and of the Son, and of the Holy Spirit, teaching
them to observe all things that I have commanded you; and Lo, I
AM with you always, even to the end of the age." AMEN.
{Matthew 28:18-20/NKJV}

The Great Commission is a call for Christians, not just limited to the clergy, for we are all called to share the love of Christ. We can do this in different creative ways, such as sharing our testimony, being a witness for Christ in our workplace, marketplace, in our communities, schools, seeking opportunity to serve others. It shouldn't be treated as an option, but more like a commandment, our mission here on earth. By fulfilling this Great Co-mission, together we can make a difference; bring hope, healing and salvation to a world which desperately needs Jesus.

BAM~Incorporated

"Fight the Good Fight!"
BAM, initially Born-Again Ministries
Has evolved into an acronym for other facets of ministry:
Be A Mentor / Becoming A Man / Broken Angry Men
Mentoring the Youth
Discipling Young Men
Sponsoring Men in Transition
From Brokenness to Wholeness
Master of the Way Federation
A Sports Program which utilizes Boxing and Martial Arts
As a sanctified vehicle to Discipline and Train Up this Generation ~
In the Way of the Master.

"GOD has blessed me with the gift of CREATIVE COMMUNICATION, and like The Psalmist David, I too have a heart after GOD's own Heart, where I love to express myself in Drama, Poetry, Music, Song, and Dance.
I also have been skilled in the ART OF WAR.
As a WATCHMAN of GOD and an Agent of Reconciliation, I have been called to be a MIGHTY PRAYER WARRIOR in The Spirit.
It has manifested in the physical realm actively practicing and teaching Martial Arts.
I am offering my talents around my forte, utilizing this as a vehicle to present the Gospel and minister ...
The Word to this Generation."

TRANSITION

For such a time as this, I believe GOD can and will sanctify this concept **for His Glory!** A practical, productive, physical outlet to enable one to release pent-up anger, aggression, and frustration, not only in today's troubled youth but in adults as well. Helping to serve as a psychological tool in building up one's esteem, control, and confidence. First and foremost, in GOD, where all our needs can and will be met...

Physically, mentally, as well as spiritually.

GOD is the motivating force that helps one achieve balance, by building one's body, while challenging one's mind, and reviving one's spirit. Where GOD's Holy Spirit ultimately leads us to inescapably realize the Truth, that one can only be truly complete in the One True Living GOD, through His Son, and by the Spirit of the Living Christ.

Making Him LORD and Master of our all, surrendering ourselves unconditionally and without reservation, thus being Saved, not just rehabilitated but regenerated in our innermost being. Redeemed, Transformed, and Refined by the renewing of the spirit of our mind.
{According to Romans 12:2}

Chaplain Nelson Colón

Honoring Our Veterans

{Collage by Adrian Rodriguez}

NELSON COLÓN

YouTube Channel
New Creation Concepts
Facebook
Chaplain NC
BAM Combat Club
Master of the Way Federation
The WATCHMEN
New Creation Concepts
NewCreationConcepts@proton.me

NewCreation Concepts

TRANSITION

His Majesty is Returning...

Are You Ready?

[1] Slipper

[2] A concrete mezzanine common in the Caribbean.

[3] Spanish for "Look, this boy is outside naked, dammit!"

[4] Spanish for Aunt.

[5] "Eat boy, before your food gets cold!"

[6] Cod Fish

[7] Tropical Root vegetables; referred to as "Vianda"

[8] Minced Garlic

[9] Fried Plantains

[10] Garlic Dipping Sauce

[11] https://kidsongs.com/lyrics/los-pollitos.html/

[12] "Island of my Infancy"

[13] Originally attributed to Saint Bernard of Clairvaux

[14] a men's summer shirt, called "The suit of the Tropics"

[15] Chicken Fricassee

[16] the island of enchantment

[17] Auntie

[18] "Today is the day, Wake up! You don't want to be late for your first day of school."

[19] "Careful!"

[20] Spanish for "We are moving."

[21] Spanish for Dad

[22] Spanish for Living Room

[23] "Let's Go, let's go!"

[24] Proverbs 16:27-29 / The Living Bible

[25] **"Fire and Rain"**: a song written and performed by James Taylor and released in 1970 on Warner Bros. Records

[26] "My son"- Translated into Conjoined Spanish Slang

[27] ***The Little Prince**: a beloved novella by the French writer, poet, and aviator Antoine de Saint-Exupery written in 1943

TRANSITION

[28] **Rosemary's Baby**: a 1968 American psychological horror film written and directed by Roman Polanski

[29] "Don't leave him alone. Take Care of him ... Your son needs you."

[30] "OMG! You are soaked in sweat. Come drink some water."

[31] "The Town" in Spanish

[32] a slower-tempo dance of Cuban origin

[33] Someone without shame

[34] **One Flew Over the Cuckoo's Nest** is a 1975 American psychological[1] comedy-drama film directed by Miloš Forman[2]

[35] **Bridge over Troubled Water:** the fifth and final studio album by the American folk-rock duo Simon & Garfunkel. Released in January 1970 on Columbia Records

[36]2 Timothy 1:7

[37] The **Lollipop Guild**: Special Munchkins who welcomed Dorothy Gale to **Oz** with a song and dance in the 1939 Classic
"The Wizard of Oz"

[38] Psalm 30:5

[39] 1 Peter 1:8

[40] **The Cross and the Switchblade** is a biographical[3] book written by the late Rev. David Wilkerson[4] with John and Elizabeth Sherrill[5], published by Bernard Geis Associates[6] in 1963

[41] "Yes my son, why not!"

[42] Matthew 12:45

[43] "Look, this is a New Yorican like you!"

[44] "Look Pop, it's a cowboy movie!"

[45] 1 John 1:7

[46] "The Lord loves you and came not to condemn, but to forgive you. So do I, love and forgive you, Papi."

---

1. https://en.wikipedia.org/wiki/Psychological_drama

2. https://en.wikipedia.org/wiki/Milo%C5%A1_Forman

3. https://en.wikipedia.org/wiki/Biographical

4. https://en.wikipedia.org/wiki/David_Wilkerson

5. https://en.wikipedia.org/wiki/John_and_Elizabeth_Sherrill

6. https://en.wikipedia.org/wiki/Bernard_Geis_Associates

[47] "The Street of the Cotto's."

www.ingramcontent.com/pod-product-compliance
Lightning Source LLC
LaVergne TN
LVHW051228080426
835513LV00016B/1467